Financial Markets and Institutions

Madura

CENGAGE
Learning™

Australia • Brazil • Japan • Korea • Mexico • Singapore • Spain • United Kingdom • United States

CENGAGE
Learning™

Financial Markets and Institutions

Madura

Executive Editors:
Michele Baird

Maureen Staudt

Michael Stranz

Project Development Manager:
Linda deStefano

Senior Marketing Coordinators:
Sara Mercurio

Lindsay Shapiro

Senior Production / Manufacturing Manager:
Donna M. Brown

PreMedia Services Supervisor:
Rebecca A. Walker

Rights & Permissions Specialist:
Kalina Hintz

Cover Image:
Getty Images*

* Unless otherwise noted, all cover images used by Custom Solutions, a part of Cengage Learning, have been supplied courtesy of Getty Images with the exception of the Earthview cover image, which has been supplied by the National Aeronautics and Space Administration (NASA).

For product information and technology assistance, contact us at
Cengage Learning Customer & Sales Support, 1-800-354-9706

For permission to use material from this text or product,
submit all requests online at **cengage.com/permissions**
Further permissions questions can be emailed to
permissionrequest@cengage.com

ISBN-13: 978-0-324-69006-4

ISBN-10: 0-324-69006-1

Cengage Learning
5191 Natorp Boulevard
Mason, Ohio 45040
USA

Cengage Learning is a leading provider of customized learning solutions with office locations around the globe, including Singapore, the United Kingdom, Australia, Mexico, Brazil, and Japan. Locate your local office at: **international.cengage.com/region**

Cengage Learning products are represented in Canada by Nelson Education, Ltd.

For your lifelong learning solutions, visit **custom.cengage.com**

Visit our corporate website at **cengage.com**

Printed in the United States of America

Acknowledgements

The content of this text has been adapted from the following product(s):

Financial Markets & Institutions (component/book only)
MADURA ISBN-10: (0-324-31946-0)
ISBN-13: (978-0-324-31946-0)

Table Of Contents

Role of Financial Markets and Institutions

A **financial market** is a market in which financial assets (securities) such as stocks and bonds can be purchased or sold. Funds are transferred in financial markets when one party purchases financial assets previously held by another party. Financial markets facilitate the flow of funds and thereby allow financing and investing by households, firms, and government agencies. This chapter provides a background on financial markets and the financial institutions that participate in them.

The specific objectives of this chapter are to:

■ describe the types of financial markets that accommodate various transactions,

■ introduce the concept of security valuation within financial markets,

■ describe the role of financial institutions within financial markets, and

■ identify the types of financial institutions that facilitate transactions in financial markets.

Overview of Financial Markets

Financial markets transfer funds from those who have excess funds to those who need funds. They enable college students to obtain student loans, families to obtain mortgages, businesses to finance their growth, and governments to finance their expenditures. Without financial markets, many students could not go to college, many families could not purchase a home, corporations could not grow, and the government could not provide as many public services. Households and businesses that supply funds to financial markets earn a return on their investment; the return is necessary to ensure that funds are supplied to the financial markets. If funds were not supplied, the financial markets would not be able to transfer funds to those who need them.

The main participants in financial markets can be classified as households, businesses, and government agencies. Those participants who provide funds to the financial markets are called **surplus units.** Households are the main type of surplus unit. Participants who use financial markets to obtain funds are called **deficit units.** Many deficit units issue (sell) securities to surplus units in order to obtain funds. A security is a certificate that represents a claim on the issuer.

The U.S. Treasury relies heavily on the financial markets to obtain funds and thus serves as a major deficit unit. It issues Treasury securities in the financial markets, which are purchased by households and other surplus units. These securities are a form of debt. They specify a maturity date when the Treasury will repay the surplus units who are holding the securities. Some businesses also issue debt securities. Other businesses issue stocks, which allow investors to become part owners of the business.

Types of Financial Markets

Each financial market is created to satisfy particular preferences of market participants. For example, some participants may want to invest funds for a short-term period, whereas others want to invest for a long-term period. Some participants are willing to tolerate a high level of risk when investing, whereas others need to avoid risk. Some participants that need funds prefer to borrow, whereas others prefer to issue stock. There are many different types of financial markets, and each market can be distinguished by the maturity structure and trading structure of its securities.

Money versus Capital Markets The financial markets that facilitate the transfer of debt securities are commonly classified by the maturity of the securities. Those financial markets that facilitate the flow of short-term funds (with maturities of less than one year) are known as **money markets,** while those that facilitate the flow of long-term funds are known as **capital markets.**

Primary versus Secondary Markets Whether referring to money market securities or capital market securities, it is necessary to distinguish between transactions in the primary market and transactions in the secondary market. **Primary markets** facilitate the issuance of new securities, while **secondary markets** facilitate the trading of existing securities. Primary market transactions provide funds to the initial issuer of securities; secondary market transactions do not. The issuance of new corporate stock or new Treasury securities is a primary market transaction, while the sale of existing corporate stock or Treasury security holdings by any business or individual is a secondary market transaction.

An important characteristic of securities that are traded in secondary markets is **liquidity,** which is the degree to which securities can easily be liquidated (sold) without a loss of value. Some securities have an active secondary market, meaning that there are many willing buyers and sellers of the security at a given point in time. Investors prefer liquid securities so that they can easily sell the securities whenever they want (without a loss in value). If a security is illiquid, investors may not be able to find a willing buyer for it in the secondary market and may have to sell the security at a large discount just to attract a buyer.

Organized versus Over-the-Counter Markets Some secondary stock market transactions occur at an **organized exchange,** or a visible marketplace for secondary market transactions. The New York Stock Exchange and American Stock Exchange are organized exchanges for secondary stock market transactions. Other financial market transactions occur in the **over-the-counter (OTC) market,** which is a telecommunications network.

Knowledge of Financial Markets Is Power Knowledge of financial markets can enhance financial decisions. Financial market participants must decide which financial markets to use to achieve their investment goals or obtain needed financing.

Securities Traded in Financial Markets

Securities can be classified as money market securities, capital market securities, or derivative securities. Each type of security tends to have specific return and risk characteristics, as described in detail in the chapters covering financial markets. The term *risk* is used here to represent the uncertainty surrounding the expected return.

Money Market Securities

Money market securities are debt securities that have a maturity of one year or less. They generally have a relatively high degree of liquidity. Money market securities tend to have a low expected return but also a low degree of risk. Various types of money market securities are listed in the top section of Exhibit 1.1, and capital market securities are listed in the bottom section.

EXHIBIT 1.1 Summary of Popular Securities

Money Market Securities	Issued by	Common Investors	Common Maturities	Secondary Market Activity
Treasury bills	Federal government	Households, firms, and financial institutions	13 weeks, 26 weeks, 1 year	High
Retail certificates of deposit (CDs)	Banks and savings institutions	Households	7 days to 5 years or longer	Nonexistent
Negotiable certificates of deposit (NCDs)	Large banks and savings institutions	Firms	2 weeks to 1 year	Moderate
Commercial paper	Bank holding companies, finance companies, and other companies	Firms	1 day to 270 days	Low
Eurodollar deposits	Banks located outside the U.S.	Firms and governments	1 day to 1 year	Nonexistent
Banker's acceptances	Banks (exporting firms can sell the acceptances at a discount to obtain funds)	Firms	30 days to 270 days	High
Federal funds	Depository institutions	Depository institutions	1 day to 7 days	Nonexistent
Repurchase agreements	Firms and financial institutions	Firms and financial institutions	1 day to 15 days	Nonexistent
Capital Market Securities				
Treasury notes and bonds	Federal government	Households, firms, and financial institutions	3 to 30 years	High
Municipal bonds	State and local governments	Households and firms	10 to 30 years	Moderate
Corporate bonds	Firms	Households and firms	10 to 30 years	Moderate
Mortgages	Individuals and firms	Financial institutions	15 to 30 years	Moderate
Equity securities	Firms	Households and firms	No maturity	High (for stocks of large firms)

Capital Market Securities

Securities with a maturity of more than one year are called **capital market securities.** Three common types of capital market securities are bonds, mortgages, and stocks.

Bonds and Mortgages Bonds are long-term debt obligations issued by corporations and government agencies to support their operations. Mortgages are long-term debt obligations created to finance the purchase of real estate.

Bonds provide a return to investors in the form of interest income (coupon payments) every six months. Since bonds and mortgages represent debt, they specify the amount and timing of interest and principal payments to investors who purchase them. At maturity, investors holding the debt securities are paid the principal. Debt securities can be sold in the secondary market if investors do not want to hold them until maturity. Since the prices of debt securities can change over time, investors may be able to enhance their return by selling the securities for a higher price than they paid for them.

Some debt securities are risky because the issuer could default on its obligation to repay the debt. Under these circumstances, the debt security will not provide the entire amount of coupon payments and principal that was promised. Long-term debt securities tend to have a higher expected return than money market securities, but they have more risk as well.

Stocks Stocks (also referred to as equity securities) are certificates representing partial ownership in the corporations that issued them. They are classified as capital market securities because they have no maturity and therefore serve as a long-term source of funds. Some corporations provide income to their stockholders by distributing a portion of their quarterly earnings in the form of dividends. Other corporations retain and reinvest all of their earnings, which allows them more potential for growth.

Equity securities differ from debt securities in that they represent partial ownership. As corporations grow and increase in value, the value of the stock increases, and investors can earn a capital gain from selling the stock for a higher price than they paid for it. Thus, investors can earn a return from stocks in the form of periodic dividends (if there are any) and a capital gain when they sell the stock. However, investors can experience a negative return if the corporation performs poorly and its stock price declines over time as a result. Equity securities have a higher expected return than most long-term debt securities, but they also exhibit a higher degree of risk.

Derivative Securities

In addition to money market and capital market securities, derivative securities are also traded in financial markets. **Derivative securities** are financial contracts whose values are derived from the values of underlying assets (such as debt securities or equity securities). Many derivative securities enable investors to engage in speculation and risk management.

Speculation Derivative securities allow an investor to speculate on movements in the underlying assets without having to purchase those assets. Some derivative securities allow investors to benefit from an increase in the value of debt securities, while others allow investors to benefit from a decrease in the value of debt securities. Similarly,

http://www.cboe.com
Information about
derivative securities.

investors can use different types of derivative securities to benefit from an increase or a decline in the value of equity securities. Since derivative securities allow investors to speculate on movements in underlying assets without purchasing the assets, they enable investors to take a large investment position without a large initial outlay and therefore to have a high degree of financial leverage. As a result of this financial leverage, the returns from investing in derivative securities are more pronounced than from simply investing in the underlying assets themselves. Investors who speculate in derivative contracts can achieve higher returns than if they had speculated in the underlying assets, but they are also exposed to higher risk.

Risk Management Derivative securities can be used in a manner that will generate gains if the value of the underlying assets declines. Consequently, financial institutions and other firms can use derivative securities to adjust the risk of their existing investments in securities. If a firm maintains investments in bonds, for example, it can take specific positions in derivative securities that will generate gains if bond values decline. In this way, derivative securities can be used to reduce a firm's risk. The loss on the bonds is offset by the gains on these derivative securities.

ILLUSTRATION Exhibit 1.2 shows how derivative securities can be combined with an investment in securities to change the investor's return and risk characteristics. Weber Inc. invests in securities that reflect the particular return and risk levels represented by Point A. If Weber desires to increase its potential return, it can take a specific position in derivative securities that will enhance its returns if the securities it has invested in perform well. If those securities perform poorly, however, the position in derivative securities will magnify any losses that occur. Thus, this derivative position pushes the firm's return-risk characteristics to Point B on the exhibit. Alternatively, Weber can take the opposite position in derivative securities; if Weber's investment securities perform poorly, this derivative position will generate a gain, offsetting the losses on the securities. However, this derivative position will likely generate a loss if the securities experience a gain. Consequently, this derivative position limits Weber's losses or gains, so the firm's return-risk characteristics resulting from this position are represented by Point C in the exhibit.

EXHIBIT 1.2

How Derivatives Can Be Used to Alter an Investor's Return and Risk Characteristics

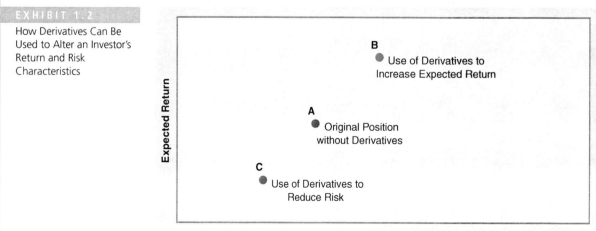

Valuation of Securities in Financial Markets

Each type of security generates a unique stream of expected cash flows to investors. As mentioned earlier, investors holding securities may receive periodic (coupon or dividend) payments and also receive a payment when they sell the securities. In addition, each security has a unique level of uncertainty surrounding the expected cash flows that it will provide to investors and therefore surrounding its return. The valuation of a security is measured as the present value of its expected cash flows, discounted at a rate that reflects the uncertainty. Since the cash flows and the uncertainty surrounding the cash flows for each security are unique, the value of each security is unique.

Market Pricing of Securities

Securities are priced in the market according to how they are valued by market participants.

ILLUSTRATION Nike stock provides cash flows to investors in the form of quarterly dividends and its stock price at the time investors sell the stock. Both the future dividends and the future stock price are uncertain. Thus, the cash flows that Nike stock will provide to investors in the future are also uncertain. Investors can attempt to estimate the future cash flows that they will receive by obtaining information that may indicate Nike's future performance, such as reports about the athletic shoe industry, announcements by Nike about its recent sales, and published opinions about Nike's management ability. The valuation process is illustrated in Exhibit 1.3.

Impact of Information on Valuations Although all investors rely on valuation to make investment decisions, different investors may derive different valuations of a security based on the existing set of information. That is, investors interpret and use information in different ways. Some investors may rely mostly on economic or industry

EXHIBIT 1.3

Use of Information to Make
Investment Decisions

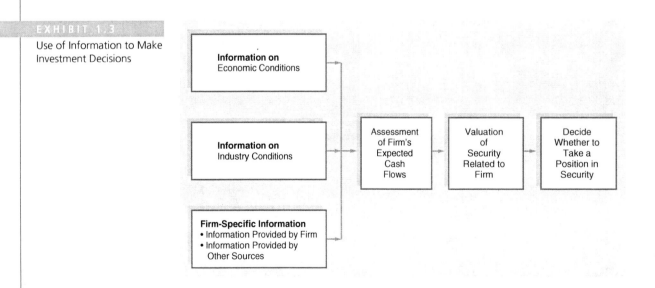

information to value a security, while others may rely on published opinions about the firm's management. Each security has an equilibrium market price at which the demand for that security is equal to the supply of that security for sale. Yet, because investors derive different values for a particular security, they do not necessarily agree that the market price is appropriate. Investors commonly take a position in a security when their assessment of its value differs from the market valuation. Thus, as shown in Exhibit 1.3, investors determine whether to take a position in a security by first using information to estimate expected cash flows, and then develop their own valuation.

Impact of Valuations on Pricing When investors receive new information that clearly indicates the likelihood of higher cash flows or less uncertainty, they revise all of their valuations of that security upward. Consequently, the prevailing price is no longer in equilibrium, as most investors now view the security as undervalued at that price. The demand for the security increases at that price, and the supply of that security for sale decreases. As a result, the market price rises to a new equilibrium level.

Conversely, when investors receive unfavorable information, they reduce the expected cash flows or increase the discount rate used in valuation. All of the valuations of the security are revised downward, which results in shifts in the demand and supply conditions and a decline in the equilibrium price.

As time passes, new information about economic conditions and corporate performance becomes available. Investors quickly attempt to assess how this information will influence the values of securities. As investors buy or sell in response to this information, security prices reach a new equilibrium. Some information has an immediate impact on security prices because market participants take positions in securities as soon as the information is released.

Announcements that do not contain any new valuable information will not elicit a market response. In some cases, market participants take their position in anticipation of a particular announcement. If the announcement was fully anticipated, there will be no market response to the announcement.

Impact of the Internet on the Valuation Process The Internet has improved the valuation of securities in several ways. Prices of securities are quoted online and can be obtained at any given moment by investors. The actual sequence of transactions is provided for some securities. Much more information about the firms that issue securities is available online, which allows securities to be priced more accurately. Furthermore, orders to buy or sell many types of securities can be submitted online, which expedites the adjustment in security prices to new information.

Market Efficiency

Because securities have market-determined prices, their favorable or unfavorable characteristics as perceived by the market are reflected in their prices. When security prices fully reflect all available information, the markets for these securities are said to be efficient. When markets are inefficient, investors can use available information ignored by the market to earn abnormally high returns on their investments.

Even if markets are efficient, this does not imply that individual or institutional investors should ignore the various investment instruments available. Investors differ with respect to the risk they are willing to incur, the desired liquidity of securities, and their tax status, making some types of securities more desirable to some investors than to others.

Some securities that are not as safe and liquid as desired may still be considered if the potential return is sufficiently high. Investors normally attempt to balance the objective of high return with their particular preference for low risk and adequate liquidity. When financial markets are efficient, any relevant information pertaining to risk will be reflected in the prices of securities.

Impact of Asymmetric Information

Much of the information used to value securities issued by firms is provided by the managers of those firms. A firm's managers possess information about its financial condition that is not necessarily available to investors. This situation is referred to as asymmetric information. The gap between the information known by managers and the information available to investors can be reduced if managers frequently disclose financial data and information to the public. Firms that have publicly traded stock are required to disclose financial information. Investors commonly rely on financial statements provided by the managers. Alternatively, they may rely on opinions by financial experts, but these opinions may be based on financial statements that were created by the firm's managers. The accounting process plays a key role in the valuation process because investors use accounting reports of a firm's revenue and expenses as a base for estimating its future cash flows. Since investors commonly use a firm's cash flows to estimate its value, the valuation process is influenced by the financial statements that are used to derive cash flow estimates.

Even when information is disclosed, however, an asymmetric information problem may still exist if some of the information provided by the firm's managers cannot be trusted. Accounting guidelines contain some flexibility that may allow unscrupulous managers to manipulate a firm's financial statements. The financial statements of firms with publicly traded stock must be audited once a year by certified public accountants. Nevertheless, there have been many cases in which a firm's earnings were overestimated, but this was not detected until the following year. Under conditions of asymmetric information, securities may be mispriced simply because the investors are using incomplete information provided by the firm's managers. Although the Internet makes information more accessible, it cannot correct misleading information provided by a firm's managers. A possible solution to the asymmetric information problem is more stringent regulations that penalize any parties who are responsible for disclosing misleading financial information, as discussed in the following section.

Financial Market Regulation

In general, securities markets are regulated to ensure that the participants are treated fairly. Many regulations were enacted in response to fraudulent practices before the Great Depression.

Disclosure

Since the use of incorrect information can result in poor investment decisions, many regulations attempt to ensure that businesses disclose accurate information. The Securities Act of 1933 was intended to ensure complete disclosure of relevant financial information on publicly offered securities and to prevent fraudulent practices in selling these securities. The Securities Exchange Act of 1934 extended the disclosure requirements to secondary market issues. It also declared illegal a variety of deceptive practices, such as misleading financial statements and trading strategies designed to manipulate the market price. In addition, it established the Securities and Exchange Commission (SEC) to oversee the securities markets, and the SEC has implemented additional laws over time. Securities laws do not prevent investors from making poor investment decisions but only attempt to ensure full disclosure of information and thus protect against fraud.

As explained earlier, a security's market price is driven by new information that affects its valuation. When information is disclosed to only a small set of investors, those investors have a major advantage over other investors. Even with regulatory oversight, cases continue to occur in which some investors had an unfair advantage because they had better access to information. Regulations are frequently refined to ensure equal access to disclosure by firms that have issued securities.

Regulatory Response to Financial Scandals

The Enron, WorldCom, and other financial scandals in the 2001–2002 period proved that the existing regulations were not sufficient to prevent fraud. Enron misled investors by exaggerating its earnings. It also failed to disclose relevant information that would have adversely affected its stock price. By the time the information became public, many of Enron's executives had sold off their holdings of Enron stock. They were able to sell the stock at a relatively high price because the negative information was withheld from the public. WorldCom also misled its investors by exaggerating its earnings. Participants in the financial markets were shocked by the degree to which these firms were able to distort their financial statements before the adverse information became public.

Many financial market participants had presumed that financial statements were accurate. In some cases, the auditors who were hired to ensure that a firm's financial statements were accurate were not meeting their responsibility. As a result, executives were able to sell their stock before most financial market participants were aware of the firm's real financial condition.

In response to the financial scandals, various regulators imposed new rules requiring firms to provide more complete and accurate financial information. They also imposed more restrictions to ensure proper auditing by auditors and proper oversight by the firm's board of directors. These rules were intended to regain the trust of investors who supply the funds to the financial markets. Through these measures, regulators tried to eliminate or reduce the asymmetric information problem and alleviate suspicions that surplus units (investors) have about the information provided by deficit units (firms). Consequently, surplus units may be more willing to supply funds in the future.

Other Regulations

In addition to the markets themselves, financial institutions participating in these markets are also regulated. Some regulations apply to all financial institutions, while others are applicable only to a specific type. Historically, regulations limited the types of financial services that any financial firm could offer. In recent years, however, many of these regulations have been removed. Details on regulations are provided throughout the text.

The performance of various financial institutions is linked to regulation. In regulating any type of financial institution, regulators face a tradeoff: they must try to impose enough regulation to ensure safety without imposing so many rules that they reduce competition and efficiency.

Global Financial Markets

Financial markets are continuously being developed throughout the world to improve the transfer of funds from surplus units to deficit units. In some countries, the financial markets are just starting to be developed. In others, such as the United States, the financial markets are being transformed to remove inefficiencies. Because the financial markets are much more developed in some countries than in others, they vary among countries in terms of the volumes of funds that are transferred from surplus units to deficit units and the types of funding that are available.

How Financial Markets Influence Economic Development

Many foreign countries have recently converted to market-oriented economies, in which businesses are created to accommodate the needs or preferences of consumers. A market economy requires the development of financial markets, where businesses can obtain the financing they need to produce products and consumers can obtain the financing they need to purchase specific products.

Before 1990, many countries in Eastern Europe had very limited opportunities for surplus units and deficit units. Consequently, private businesses did not have access to funds and could not expand. In addition, households did not have access to funds and could not purchase homes. Businesses were mostly owned by the government and had to rely on government funding. Since 1990, the governments of these countries have allowed for **privatization,** or the sale of government-owned firms to individuals. In addition, some businesses have issued stock, which allows many other investors who do not work in the business to participate in the ownership. Financial markets have been established in these countries to ensure that these businesses can obtain funding from surplus units. With these changes, private businesses are now able to obtain funds by borrowing or by issuing stock to investors. Surplus units have the opportunity to provide credit (loans) to some businesses or become stockholders of other businesses.

Global Integration

Many financial markets are globally integrated, allowing participants to move funds out of one country's markets and into another's. Foreign investors serve as key surplus units in the United States by purchasing U.S. Treasury securities and other types of securities issued by businesses. Conversely, some investors based in the United States serve as key surplus units for foreign countries by purchasing securities issued by foreign corporations and government agencies. In addition, investors assess the potential return and the risk of securities in financial markets across countries and invest in the market that satisfies their return and risk preferences.

With these more integrated financial markets, U.S. market movements may have a greater impact on foreign market movements, and vice versa. Because interest rates are influenced by the supply of and demand for available funds, they are now more susceptible to foreign lending or borrowing activities.

Barriers to Global Integration Although the global integration of financial markets has increased, various barriers still exist. Some barriers may restrict the transfer of funds to a foreign financial market. One barrier is the lack of information about foreign companies in which investors would like to invest. The Internet has made this type of information much more accessible in recent years, but the information that is available may not be standardized across countries. For example, each country imposes its own accounting regulations regarding how businesses report their financial condition. Consequently, investors may have difficulty interpreting the financial statements provided by businesses in other countries.

Another barrier is the excessive cost of executing international transactions in financial markets. These transactions tend to require more effort by the intermediaries and therefore are more costly to the surplus or deficit units that wish to invest or obtain funds internationally. The transaction costs have declined substantially with the use of electronic communications, but are still higher than for domestic transactions.

Financial Market Integration within Europe The most pronounced progress in global financial market integration has occurred in Europe. Historically, the financial markets in each country in Western Europe were well developed but isolated from those of other countries. Even when no laws prohibited transactions outside the country, differences in tax laws and other regulations complicated international transactions. In the 1980s and 1990s, however, numerous regulations were eliminated so that surplus and deficit units in one European country could use financial markets throughout Europe. Some stock exchanges in different European countries merged, making it easier for investors to conduct all of their stock transactions on one exchange. Since 1999, the adoption of the euro as the currency by 12 European countries (the so-called eurozone) has encouraged more financial market integration within Europe because all securities issued within these countries are now denominated in the euro. Thus, investors in any of these countries do not have to convert their currency.

Role of the Foreign Exchange Market

International financial transactions (except for those within the eurozone) normally require the exchange of currencies. The **foreign exchange market** facilitates the exchange of currencies. Many commercial banks and other financial institutions serve as intermediaries in the foreign exchange market. They serve as brokers by matching up participants who want to exchange one currency for another. Some of these financial institutions also serve as dealers by taking positions in currencies to accommodate foreign exchange requests.

ILLUSTRATION O'Hara Bank of Chicago receives requests by corporations to exchange dollars for Japanese yen (the Japanese currency). It also receives requests by other corporations to exchange yen for dollars. At a given point in time, the bank's ask quote for yen (the price at which it is willing to sell yen) is slightly higher than its bid quote (the price at which it is willing to purchase yen). Thus, the bank earns a profit when it accepts yen from one corporation and provides them to another corporation. It also provides this service for several other currencies.

The bank may also serve as a dealer when a corporation requests a currency exchange that cannot be offset by requests by other corporations. For instance, a Mexican company wants to exchange its pesos for U.S. dollars to purchase supplies from a U.S. firm. O'Hara Bank currently has no customers that need pesos. It accommodates the Mexican company's request and now has pesos. The bank could benefit from this position if the market value of the Mexican peso rises over time. Conversely, it could incur a loss from this position if the market value of the peso declines.

Foreign Exchange Rates Like securities, most currencies have a market-determined price (exchange rate) that changes in response to supply and demand conditions. If there is a sudden shift in the aggregate demand by corporations, government agencies, and individuals for a given currency, or a shift in the aggregate supply of that currency for sale (to be exchanged), the price will change.

ILLUSTRATION Yesterday, several banks that accommodate the exchange between Mexican pesos and U.S. dollars experienced more requests from customers wanting to exchange pesos for dollars than from customers wanting to exchange dollars for pesos. Consequently, many of the banks are now holding larger inventories of pesos than they desire. They decide to reduce their price for pesos in an attempt to discourage future customer requests to exchange pesos for dollars. At the lower price, the customers would now receive fewer dollars for a given amount of pesos.

Role of Financial Institutions in Financial Markets

If financial markets were **perfect,** all information about any securities for sale in primary and secondary markets (including the creditworthiness of the security issuer) would be continuously and freely available to investors. In addition, all information identifying investors interested in purchasing securities as well as investors planning to sell securities would be freely available. Furthermore, all securities for sale could be broken down (or unbundled) into any size desired by investors, and security transaction costs would be nonexistent. Under these conditions, financial intermediaries would not be necessary.

Because markets are **imperfect,** securities buyers and sellers do not have full access to information and cannot always break down securities to the precise size they desire. Financial institutions are needed to resolve the problems caused by market imperfections. They receive requests from surplus and deficit units on what securities are to be purchased or sold, and they use this information to match up buyers and sellers of securities. Because the amount of a specific security to be sold does not always equal the amount desired by investors, financial institutions sometimes unbundle the securities by spreading them across several investors until the entire amount is sold. Without financial institutions, the information and transaction costs of financial market transactions would be excessive.

Role of Depository Institutions

A major type of financial intermediary is the depository institution, which accepts deposits from surplus units and provides credit to deficit units through loans and purchases of securities. Depository institutions are popular financial institutions for the following reasons:

- They offer deposit accounts that can accommodate the amount and liquidity characteristics desired by most surplus units.
- They repackage funds received from deposits to provide loans of the size and maturity desired by deficit units.
- They accept the risk on loans provided.
- They have more expertise than individual surplus units in evaluating the creditworthiness of deficit units.
- They diversify their loans among numerous deficit units and therefore can absorb defaulted loans better than individual surplus units could.

To appreciate these advantages, consider the flow of funds from surplus units to deficit units if depository institutions did not exist. Each surplus unit would have to identify a deficit unit desiring to borrow the precise amount of funds available for the precise time period in which funds would be available. Furthermore, each surplus unit would have to perform the credit evaluation and incur the risk of default. Under these conditions, many surplus units would likely hold their funds rather than channel them to deficit units. Thus, the flow of funds from surplus units to deficit units would be disrupted.

When a depository institution offers a loan, it is acting as a creditor, just as if it had purchased a debt security. Yet, the more personalized loan agreement is less marketable in the secondary market than a debt security, because detailed provisions on a loan can differ significantly among loans. Any potential investors would need to review all provisions before purchasing loans in the secondary market.

A more specific description of each depository institution's role in the financial markets follows.

Commercial Banks In aggregate, commercial banks are the most dominant depository institution. They serve surplus units by offering a wide variety of deposit accounts, and they transfer deposited funds to deficit units by providing direct loans or purchasing debt securities. Commercial banks serve both the private and public sectors, as their deposit and lending services are utilized by households, businesses, and government agencies.

Savings Institutions Savings institutions, which are sometimes referred to as thrift institutions, are another type of depository institution. Savings institutions include savings and loan associations (S&Ls) and savings banks. Like commercial banks, S&Ls offer deposit accounts to surplus units and then channel these deposits to deficit units. However, S&Ls have concentrated on residential mortgage loans, whereas commercial banks have concentrated on commercial loans. This difference in the allocation of funds has caused the performance of commercial banks and S&Ls to differ significantly over time. In recent decades, however, deregulation has permitted S&Ls more flexibility in allocating their funds, causing their functions to become more similar to those of commercial banks. Although S&Ls can be owned by shareholders, most are mutual (depositor owned).

Savings banks are similar to S&Ls, except that they have more diversified uses of funds. However, this difference has narrowed over time. Like S&Ls, most savings banks are mutual.

Credit Unions Credit unions differ from commercial banks and savings institutions in that they (1) are nonprofit and (2) restrict their business to the credit union members, who share a common bond (such as a common employer or union). Because of the common bond characteristic, credit unions tend to be much smaller than other depository institutions. They use most of their funds to provide loans to their members.

Role of Nondepository Financial Institutions

Nondepository institutions generate funds from sources other than deposits but also play a major role in financial intermediation. These institutions are briefly described here.

Finance Companies Most finance companies obtain funds by issuing securities, then lend the funds to individuals and small businesses. The functions of finance companies overlap the functions of depository institutions, yet each type of institution concentrates on a particular segment of the financial markets (explained in the chapters devoted to these institutions).

Mutual Funds Mutual funds sell shares to surplus units and use the funds received to purchase a portfolio of securities. They are the dominant nondepository financial institution when measured in total assets. Some mutual funds concentrate their investment in capital market securities, such as stocks or bonds. Others, known as **money market mutual funds,** concentrate in money market securities. The minimum denomination of the types of securities purchased by mutual funds is typically greater than the savings of an individual surplus unit. By purchasing shares of mutual funds and money market mutual funds, small savers are able to invest in a diversified portfolio of securities with a relatively small amount of funds.

Securities Firms Securities firms provide a wide variety of functions in financial markets. Some securities firms use their information resources to act as a **broker,** executing securities transactions between two parties. Many financial transactions are standardized to a degree. For example, stock transactions are normally in multiples of 100 shares. To expedite the securities trading process, the delivery procedure for each security transaction is also somewhat standard.

Brokers charge a fee for executing transactions. The fee is reflected in the difference (or **spread**) between their **bid** and **ask** quotes. The markup as a percentage of the transaction amount will likely be greater for less common transactions, as more time is needed to match up buyers and sellers. It will also likely be greater for transactions of relatively small amounts in order to provide adequate compensation for the time involved in executing the transaction.

In addition to brokerage services, securities firms also provide investment banking services. Some securities firms place newly issued securities for corporations and government agencies; this task differs from traditional brokerage activities because it involves the primary market. When securities firms **underwrite** newly issued securities, they may sell the securities for a client at a guaranteed price, or they may simply sell the securities at the best price they can get for their client.

Furthermore, securities firms often act as **dealers,** making a market in specific securities by adjusting their inventory of securities. Although a broker's income is mostly based on the markup, the dealer's income is influenced by the performance of the security portfolio maintained. Some dealers also provide brokerage services and therefore earn income from both types of activities.

Another investment banking activity offered by securities firms is advisory services on mergers and other forms of corporate restructuring. Securities firms may not only help a firm plan its restructuring but also execute the change in the firm's capital structure by placing the securities issued by the firm.

Insurance Companies Insurance companies provide insurance policies to individuals and firms that reduce the financial burden associated with death, illness, and damage to property. They charge premiums in exchange for the insurance that they provide. They invest the funds that they receive in the form of premiums until the funds are needed to cover insurance claims. Insurance companies commonly invest the funds in stocks or bonds issued by corporations or in bonds issued by the government. In this way, they finance the needs of deficit units and thus serve as important financial intermediaries. Their overall performance is linked to the performance of the stocks and bonds in which they invest.

Pension Funds Many corporations and government agencies offer pension plans to their employees. The employees, their employers, or both periodically contribute funds to the plan. Pension funds provide an efficient way for individuals to save for their retirement. The pension funds manage the money until the individuals withdraw the funds from their retirement accounts. The money that is contributed to individual retirement accounts is commonly invested by the pension funds in stocks or bonds issued by corporations or in bonds issued by the government. In this way, pension funds finance the needs of deficit units and thus serve as important financial intermediaries.

Comparison of Roles among Financial Institutions

The role of financial institutions in facilitating the flow of funds from individual surplus units to deficit units is illustrated in Exhibit 1.4. Surplus units are shown on the left side of the exhibit, and deficit units are shown on the right side. Three different flows of funds from surplus units to deficit units are shown in the exhibit. One set of flows represents deposits from surplus units that are transformed by depository institutions into loans for deficit units. A second set of flows represents purchases of securities (commercial paper) issued by finance companies that are transformed into finance company loans for deficit units. A third set of flows reflects the purchases of shares issued by mutual funds, which are used by the mutual funds to purchase debt and equity securities of deficit units.

The deficit units also receive funding from insurance companies and pension funds. Because insurance companies and pension funds purchase massive amounts of stocks

EXHIBIT 1.4   Comparison of Roles among Financial Institutions

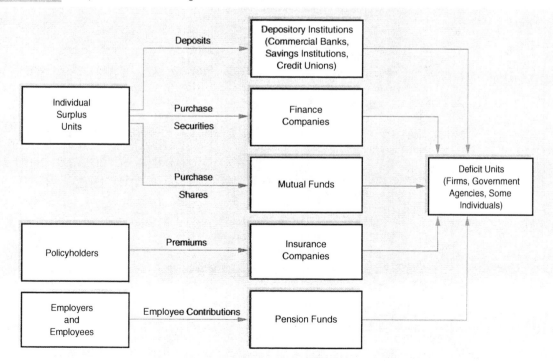

and bonds, they finance much of the expenditures made by large deficit units, such as corporations and government agencies.

Securities firms are not shown in Exhibit 1.4, but they play a very important role in facilitating the flow of funds. Many of the transactions between the financial institutions and deficit units are executed by securities firms. Furthermore, some funds flow directly from surplus units to deficit units as a result of security transactions, with securities firms serving as brokers.

Role as a Monitor of Publicly Traded Firms In addition to the roles just described, financial institutions also serve as monitors of publicly traded firms. Because insurance companies, pension funds, and some mutual funds are major investors in stocks, they can have some influence over the management of publicly traded firms. In recent years, many large institutional investors have publicly criticized the management of specific firms, which has resulted in corporate restructuring or even the firing of executives in some cases. Thus, institutional investors not only provide financial support to companies but exercise some degree of corporate control over them. By serving as activist shareholders, they can help ensure that managers of publicly held corporations are making decisions that are in the best interests of the shareholders.

Overview of Financial Institutions

Exhibit 1.5 summarizes the main sources and uses of funds for each type of financial institution. Households with savings are served by the depository institutions. Households with deficient funds are served by depository institutions and finance companies. Large corporations and governments that issue securities obtain financing from all types of financial institutions.

EXHIBIT 1.5

Summary of Institutional Sources and Uses of Funds

Financial Institutions	Main Sources of Funds	Main Uses of Funds
Commercial banks	Deposits from households, businesses, and government agencies	Purchases of government and corporate securities; loans to businesses and households
Savings institutions	Deposits from households, businesses, and government agencies	Purchases of government and corporate securities; mortgages and other loans to households; some loans to businesses
Credit unions	Deposits from credit union members	Loans to credit union members
Finance companies	Securities sold to households and businesses	Loans to households and businesses
Mutual funds	Shares sold to households, businesses, and government agencies	Purchases of long-term government and corporate securities
Money market funds	Shares sold to households, businesses, and government agencies	Purchases of short-term government and corporate securities
Insurance companies	Insurance premiums and earnings from investments	Purchases of long-term government and corporate securities
Pension funds	Employer/employee contributions	Purchases of long-term government and corporate securities

Competition between Financial Institutions

A financial institution is expected to operate in a manner that will maximize the value of its owners. The value of a financial institution is the present value of its future cash flows. Thus, its value is closely tied to its growth and profitability. In addition, its value is influenced by its degree of risk, since the required rate of return by investors in it is positively related to its risk. Managers serve as agents for the owners and should make decisions with the intention to maximize firm value. In the 1960s and 1970s, managerial decision making was limited because financial institution operations were highly specialized and constrained. There was limited competition across different types of financial institutions. Commercial banks served as the key lenders of short-term corporate funds, while securities firms helped corporations obtain long-term funds. Savings institutions specialized in mortgages, while insurance companies focused their investment in bonds.

There was also very little competition in obtaining funds during those decades. Deposits provided by surplus units to commercial banks and savings institutions were heavily regulated to prevent competition. Then, in the 1970s, the development of mutual funds created competition for funds held by surplus units. Deregulation of deposit rates in the early 1980s provided additional competition for these funds. Furthermore, in the 1980s, regulators allowed savings institutions, insurance companies, and other financial institutions to be more flexible in their use of funds. The momentum for additional flexibility continued in the 1990s. Today, many financial institutions are offering a greater variety of products and services to diversify their business. As a consequence, their services overlap more and competition has increased. Because there are different regulatory agencies for different types of financial institutions, coordination among these regulators is difficult to maintain. Differential regulations can cause some financial institutions to have a comparative advantage over others.

Impact of the Internet on Competition The Internet has promoted more intense competition among financial institutions. Some commercial banks have been created solely as online entities. Because they have lower costs, they can offer higher interest rates on deposits and lower rates on loans. Other banks also offer online services, which can reduce costs, increase efficiency, and intensify banking competition. Some insurance companies conduct much of their business online, which reduces their operating costs and forces other insurance companies to price their services competitively. Some brokerage firms conduct much of their business online, which reduces their operating costs; because these firms can lower the fees they charge, they force other brokerage firms to price their services competitively. The Internet has also made it possible for corporations and municipal governments to circumvent securities firms by conducting security offerings online and selling directly to investors. This capability forces securities firms to be more competitive in the services they offer to issuers of securities.

Consolidation of Financial Institutions

As regulations have been reduced, managers of financial institutions have more flexibility to offer services that could increase their cash flows and value. The reduction in regulations has allowed financial institutions more opportunities to capitalize on economies of scale. Commercial banks have acquired other commercial banks so that they can generate a higher volume of business supported by a given infrastructure. By increasing the volume of services produced, the average cost of providing the services (such as loans) can be reduced. Savings institutions have consolidated to achieve economies of scale for their mortgage lending business. Insurance companies have consolidated so that they can reduce the average cost of providing insurance services.

The reduction in regulations has also allowed different types of financial institutions to capitalize on economies of scope. Commercial banks have merged with savings institutions, securities firms, finance companies, mutual funds, and insurance companies. Although the operations of each type of financial institution are commonly managed separately, a financial conglomerate offers advantages to customers who prefer to obtain all of their financial services from a single financial institution.

ILLUSTRATION Consider the merger of Citicorp and Travelers Group to form Citigroup. Citicorp's business in the United States was focused on commercial banking, consumer finance, credit cards, and small business finance. Travelers Group had historically focused on life insurance and property and casualty insurance. Before the merger with Citicorp, however, it had acquired Salomon Brothers, a securities firm that provided investment banking services such as underwriting new securities issued by corporations, and Smith Barney, another securities firm that provided brokerage services.

The merger between Citicorp and Travelers resulted in a financial conglomerate worth $72 billion that offers commercial loans, advisory services for corporations planning to restructure, consumer loans, credit cards, insurance, underwriting services, brokerage services, and mutual funds. Although each type of operation within Citigroup is unique, it can benefit from its relationship with the other operations in the same financial conglomerate. For example, since the underwriting of securities normally utilizes some brokerage operations to help place newly issued securities for firms, the underwriting unit may pass some business off to the brokerage operating unit. The mutual fund unit can pass on some business to the brokerage unit to execute its security transactions. Furthermore, each unit can link its customers with the other units to provide additional services.

Several other recent mergers have also resulted in financial conglomerates. Morgan Stanley, an investment bank, acquired Dean Witter in order to expand its brokerage business. Wachovia, a commercial bank, acquired CoreStates Financial in order to expand its financial services. J.P. Morgan Chase, a commercial bank, acquired Bank One in order to expand its retail banking and credit card businesses. The combined assets of these two financial institutions exceed $1 trillion. Overall, such acquisitions have allowed financial institutions to expand their services.

Wells Fargo is a classic example of the evolution in financial services. It originally focused on commercial banking, but has expanded its nonbank services to include mortgages, small business loans, consumer loans, real estate, brokerage, investment banking, online financial services, and insurance. In a recent annual report, Wells Fargo stated:

> *Our diversity in businesses makes us much more than a bank. We're a diversified financial services company. We're competing in a highly fragmented and fast growing industry: Financial Services. This helps us weather downturns that inevitably affect any one segment of our industry.*

EXHIBIT 1.6 Organizational Structure of a Financial Conglomerate

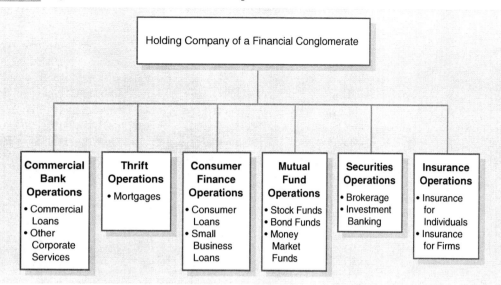

Impact of Consolidation on Valuation When managers of financial institutions pursue consolidation to achieve economies of scale or scope, they may be able to increase their firm's value by increasing cash flows (increasing revenue or reducing expenses). Alternatively, consolidation may be intended to diversify the institution's services and reduce risk. A lower level of risk allows for a reduction in the required rate of return by investors and can increase value.

Typical Structure of a Financial Conglomerate A typical organizational structure of a financial conglomerate is shown in Exhibit 1.6. Historically, each of the financial services (such as banking, mortgages, brokerage, and insurance) had significant barriers to entry, so only a limited number of firms competed in that industry. The barriers prevented most firms from offering a wide variety of these services. In recent years, the barriers to entry have been reduced, allowing firms that had specialized in one service to more easily expand into other financial services. Many firms expanded by acquiring other financial service firms. Thus, many financial conglomerates are composed of various financial institutions that were originally independent, but are now units (or subsidiaries) of the conglomerate.

An individual customer can rely on the financial conglomerate for convenient access to life and health insurance, brokerage, mutual funds, investment advice and financial planning, bank deposits, and personal loans. A corporate customer can turn to the financial conglomerate for property and casualty insurance, health insurance plans for employees, business loans, advice on restructuring its businesses, issuing new debt or equity securities, and management of its pension plan. Many financial conglomerates expect to grow by providing additional financial services to their existing customers. For example, Wells Fargo provides its 15 million customers with about one-fourth of the financial services they need (on average). Thus, it plans to pursue its existing customer base to try to provide the other three-fourths of services that are currently provided by other financial services companies.

Global Expansion by Financial Institutions

GL🌐BALASPECTS Many financial institutions have expanded internationally to capitalize on their expertise. Commercial banks, insurance companies, and securities firms have expanded through international mergers. An international merger between financial institutions enables the merged company to offer the services of both entities to its entire customer base. For example, a U.S. commercial bank may have specialized in lending while a European securities firm specialized in services such as underwriting securities. A merger between the two entities allows the U.S. bank to provide its services to the European customer base (clients of the European securities firm), while the European securities firm can offer its services to the U.S. customer base. By combining specialized skills and customer bases, the merged financial institutions can offer more services to clients and have an international customer base.

The adoption of the euro by 12 European countries has increased business between European countries and created a more competitive environment in Europe. European financial institutions, which had primarily competed with other financial institutions based in their own country, recognized that they would now face more competition from financial institutions in other countries. Consequently, many financial institutions have engaged in international mergers so that they can serve clients throughout Europe and provide a wider variety of services. By offering their services to a larger customer base, they can increase efficiency (reduce the cost) and therefore price their services more competitively.

Many financial institutions have attempted to benefit from opportunities in emerging markets. For example, Merrill Lynch and other large securities firms have expanded into many countries to offer underwriting services for firms and government agencies. The need for this service has increased most dramatically in countries where businesses have been privatized. In addition, commercial banks expanded into emerging markets to provide loans. Although lending in emerging markets can produce high returns, it is also subject to a high level of risk. The Asian crisis that began in 1997 resulted in numerous defaults on international business loans provided by financial institutions from the United States and Europe. Some financial institutions continue to offer loans in emerging markets, although not as aggressively as before the crisis.

SUMMARY

■ Financial markets facilitate the transfer of funds from surplus units to deficit units. Because funding needs vary among deficit units, various financial markets have been established. The primary market allows for the issuance of new securities, while the secondary market allows for the sale of existing securities. Money markets facilitate the sale of short-term securities, while capital markets facilitate the sale of long-term securities.

■ The valuation of a security represents the present value of future cash flows that it is expected to gener-

ate. New information that indicates a change in expected cash flows or the degree of uncertainty affects the prices of securities in financial markets. Investors monitor economic conditions and firm-specific conditions that may have an impact on expected cash flows or the degree of uncertainty surrounding securities issued by that firm.

■ Depository and nondepository institutions help to finance the needs of deficit units. Depository institutions can serve as effective intermediaries within financial markets because they have greater information on possible sources and uses of funds, they are capable of assessing the creditworthiness of borrowers, and they can repackage deposited funds in sizes and maturities desired by borrowers.

Nondepository institutions are major purchasers of securities and therefore provide funding to deficit units.

■ The main depository institutions are commercial banks, savings institutions, and credit unions. The main nondepository institutions are finance companies, mutual funds, pension funds, and insurance companies. Many financial institutions have been consolidated (due to mergers) into financial conglomerates, where they serve as subsidiaries of the conglomerate while conducting their specialized services. Thus, some financial conglomerates are able to provide all types of financial services. Consolidation allows for economies of scale and scope, which can enhance cash flows and increase the financial institution's value. In addition, consolidation can diversify the institution's services and increase value through the reduction in risk.

POINT COUNTER-POINT

Will Computer Technology Cause Financial Intermediaries to Become Extinct?

Point Yes. Financial intermediaries benefit from access to information. As information becomes more accessible, individuals will have the information they need before investing or borrowing funds. They will not need financial intermediaries to make their decisions.

Counter-Point No. Individuals rely not only on information, but also on expertise. Some financial intermediaries specialize in credit analysis so that they can make loans. Surplus units will continue to provide funds to financial intermediaries rather than make direct loans, because they are not capable of credit analysis, even if more information about prospective borrowers is available. Some financial intermediaries no longer have physical buildings for customer service, but they still require people who have the expertise to assess the creditworthiness of prospective borrowers.

Who Is Correct? Use InfoTrac or some other source search engine to learn more about this issue. Offer your own opinion on this issue.

QUESTIONS AND APPLICATIONS

1. **Surplus and Deficit Units** Explain the meaning of surplus units and deficit units. Provide an example of each. Which types of financial institutions do you deal with? Explain whether you are acting as a surplus unit or a deficit unit in your relationship with each financial institution.

2. **Types of Markets** Distinguish between primary and secondary markets. Distinguish between money and capital markets.

3. **Imperfect Markets** Distinguish between perfect and imperfect security markets. Explain why the existence of imperfect markets creates a need for financial intermediaries.

4. **Efficient Markets** Explain the meaning of efficient markets. Why might we expect markets to be efficient most of the time? In recent years, several securities firms have been guilty of using inside information when purchasing securities, thereby achieving returns well above the norm (even when accounting for risk). Does this suggest that the security markets are not efficient? Explain.

5. **Securities Laws** What was the purpose of the Securities Act of 1933? What was the purpose of the Securities Exchange Act of 1934? Do these laws prevent investors from making poor investment decisions? Explain.

6. **International Barriers** If barriers to international securities markets are reduced, will a country's interest rate be more or less susceptible to foreign lending or borrowing activities? Explain.

7. **International Flow of Funds** In what way could the international flow of funds cause a decline in interest rates?

8. **Securities Firms** What are the functions of securities firms? Many securities firms employ brokers and dealers. Distinguish between the functions of a broker and those of a dealer, and explain how each is compensated.

9. **Standardized Securities** Why is it necessary for securities to be somewhat standardized? Explain why some financial flows of funds cannot occur through the sale of standardized securities. If securities were not standardized, how would this affect the volume of financial transactions conducted by brokers?

10. **Marketability** Commercial banks use some funds to purchase securities and other funds to make loans. Why are the securities more marketable than loans in the secondary market?

11. **Depository Institutions** How have the asset compositions of savings and loan associations differed from those of commercial banks? Explain why and how this distinction may change over time.

12. **Credit Unions** With regard to the profit motive, how are credit unions different from other financial institutions?

13. **Nondepository Institutions** Compare the main sources and uses of funds for finance companies, insurance companies, and pension funds.

14. **Mutual Funds** What is the function of a mutual fund? Why are mutual funds popular among investors? How does a money market mutual fund differ from a stock or bond mutual fund?

15. **Impact of Privatization on Financial Markets** Explain how the privatization of companies in Europe can lead to the development of new securities markets.

ADVANCED QUESTIONS

16. **Comparing Financial Institutions** Classify the types of financial institutions mentioned in this chapter as either depository or nondepository. Explain the general difference between depository and nondepository institution sources of funds. It is often stated that all types of financial institutions have begun to offer services that were previously offered only by certain types. Consequently, many financial institutions are becoming more similar in terms of their operations. Yet, the performance levels still differ significantly among types of financial institutions. Why?

17. **Financial Intermediation** Look in a recent business periodical for news about a recent financial transaction that involves two financial institutions. For this transaction, determine the following:
    a. How will each institution's balance sheet be affected?
    b. Will either institution receive immediate income from the transaction?
    c. Who is the ultimate user of funds?
    d. Who is the ultimate source of funds?

18. **Role of Accounting in Financial Markets** Integrate the roles of accounting, regulations, and financial market participation. That is, explain how financial market participants rely on accounting, and why regulatory oversight of the accounting process is necessary.

INTERPRETING FINANCIAL NEWS

"Interpreting Financial News" tests your ability to comprehend common statements made by Wall Street analysts and portfolio managers who participate in the financial markets. Interpret the following statements made by Wall Street analysts and portfolio managers:

a. "The price of IBM will not be affected by the announcement that its earnings have increased as expected."

b. "The lending operations at Bank of America should benefit from strong economic growth."

c. "The brokerage and underwriting performance at Merrill Lynch should benefit from strong economic growth."

INTERNET EXERCISE

Assess the current price of the common stock of IBM, using the website http://www.nyse.com. Insert the ticker symbol "IBM" within the box called "Quick quotes."

What was the closing price on IBM's stock yesterday? From the volume graph, estimate the number of shares traded yesterday. What are the 52-week high and low prices for IBM?

MANAGING IN FINANCIAL MARKETS

Utilizing Financial Markets As a financial manager of a large firm, you plan to borrow $70 million over the next year.

a. What are the more likely alternatives for you to borrow $70 million?

b. Assuming that you decide to issue debt securities, describe the types of financial institutions that may purchase these securities.

c. How do individuals indirectly provide the financing for your firm when they maintain deposits at depository institutions, invest in mutual funds, purchase insurance policies, or invest in pensions?

FLOW OF FUNDS EXERCISE

Roles of Financial Markets and Institutions

This continuing exercise focuses on the interactions of a single manufacturing firm (Carson Company) in the financial markets. It illustrates how financial markets and institutions are integrated and facilitate the flow of funds in the business and financial environment. At the end of every chapter, this exercise provides a list of questions about Carson Company that require the application of concepts learned within the chapter, as related to the flow of funds.

Carson Company is a large manufacturing firm in California that was created 20 years ago by the Carson family. It was initially financed with an equity investment by the Carson family and 10 other individuals. Over time, Carson Company has obtained substantial loans from finance companies and commercial banks. The interest rate on the loans is tied to market interest rates and is adjusted every six months. Thus, Carson's cost of obtaining funds is sensitive to interest rate movements. It has a credit line with a bank in case it suddenly needs to obtain funds for a temporary period. It has purchased Treasury securities that it could sell if it experiences any liquidity problems.

Carson Company has assets valued at about $50 million and generates sales of about $100 million per year. Some of its growth is attributed to its acquisitions of other firms. Because of its expectations of a strong U.S. economy, Carson plans to grow in the future by expanding its business and through acquisitions. It expects that it will need substantial long-term financing and plans to borrow additional funds either through loans or by issuing bonds. It is also considering the issuance of stock to raise funds in the next year. Carson closely monitors conditions in financial markets that could affect its cash inflows and cash outflows and therefore affect its value.

a. In what way is Carson a surplus unit?

b. In what way is Carson a deficit unit?

c. How might finance companies facilitate Carson's expansion?

d. How might commercial banks facilitate Carson's expansion?

e. Why might Carson have limited access to additional debt financing during its growth phase?

f. How might investment banks facilitate Carson's expansion?

g. How might Carson use the primary market to facilitate its expansion?

h. How might it use the secondary market?

i. If financial markets were perfect, how might this have allowed Carson to avoid financial institutions?

j. The loans provided by commercial banks to Carson required that Carson receive approval from them before pursuing any large projects. What is the purpose of this condition? Does this condition benefit the owners of the company?

WSJ EXERCISE

Differentiating between Primary and Secondary Markets

Review the different tables relating to stock markets and bond markets that appear in Section C of *The Wall Street Journal*. Explain whether each of these tables is focused on the primary or secondary markets.

2

Functions of the Fed

The Federal Reserve System (the Fed), as the central bank of the United States, has the responsibility for conducting national monetary policy. Such policy influences interest rates and other economic variables that determine the prices of securities. Participants in the financial markets therefore closely monitor the Fed's monetary policy. It is important that they understand how the Fed's actions may influence security prices so that they can manage their security portfolios in response to the Fed's policies.

The specific objectives of this chapter are to:

- identify the key components of the Fed that dictate monetary policy,
- describe the tools used by the Fed to influence monetary policy,
- explain how bank regulation in the early 1980s affected monetary policy, and
- explain how monetary policy is used in other countries.

Organization of the Fed

The First Bank of the United States was created in 1791 to oversee the commercial banking system and attempt to maintain a stable economy. Because its 20-year charter was not renewed by Congress, the First Bank was terminated in 1811. A major criticism of the bank was that it interfered with the development of the banking system and economic growth. Its termination, however, reduced public confidence in the banking system. In 1816 the Second Bank of the United States was established, and because its 20-year charter also was not renewed by Congress, it was terminated in 1836.

During the late 1800s and early 1900s, several banking panics occurred, culminating with a major crisis in 1907. This motivated another attempt to establish a central bank. Accordingly, in 1913 the Federal Reserve Act was passed, establishing reserve requirements for those commercial banks that desired to become members. It also specified 12 districts across the United States as well as a city in each district where a Federal Reserve district bank was to be established. Each district bank had the ability to buy and sell government securities, which could affect the money supply (as will be explained later in this chapter). Each district bank focused on its particular district, without much concern for other districts. Over time, the system became more centralized, and money supply decisions were assigned to a particular group of individuals rather than across 12 district banks.

The Fed earns most of its income in the form of interest on its holdings of U.S. government securities (to be discussed shortly). It also earns some income from providing services to financial institutions. Most of its income is transferred to the Treasury.

The Fed is involved (along with other agencies) in regulating commercial banks. It also conducts monetary policy, adjusting the money supply in an attempt to achieve full employment and price stability (low or zero inflation) in the United States.

- The Fed as it exists today has five major components:
- Federal Reserve district banks
- Member banks
- Board of Governors
- Federal Open Market Committee (FOMC)
- Advisory committees

Federal Reserve District Banks

The 12 Federal Reserve districts are identified in Exhibit 4.1, along with the city where each district bank is located and the district branches. The New York district bank is considered the most important because many large banks are located in this district. Commercial banks that become members of the Fed are required to purchase stock in their **Federal Reserve district bank.** This stock, which is not traded in a secondary market, pays a maximum dividend of 6 percent annually.

Each Fed district bank has nine directors. Six are elected by member banks in that district. Of these six directors, three are professional bankers and three are businesspeople. The other three directors are appointed by the Board of Governors (to be discussed shortly). The nine directors appoint the president of their Fed district bank.

Fed district banks facilitate operations within the banking system by clearing checks, replacing old currency, and providing loans (through the discount window) to depository institutions in need of funds. They also collect economic data and conduct research projects on commercial banking and economic trends.

Member Banks

Commercial banks can elect to become member banks if they meet specific requirements of the Board of Governors. All national banks (chartered by the Comptroller of the Currency) are required to be members of the Fed, but other banks (chartered by their respective states) are not. Currently, about 35 percent of all banks are members; these banks account for about 70 percent of all bank deposits.

Board of Governors

The **Board of Governors** (sometimes called the Federal Reserve Board) is made up of seven individual members with offices in Washington, D.C. Each member is appointed by the president of the United States (and confirmed by the Senate) and serves a nonrenewable 14-year term. This long term is thought to reduce political pressure on the governors and thus encourage the development of policies that will benefit the U.S. economy over the long run. The terms are staggered so that one term expires in every even-numbered year.

EXHIBIT 4.1 Locations of Federal Reserve District Banks and Branches

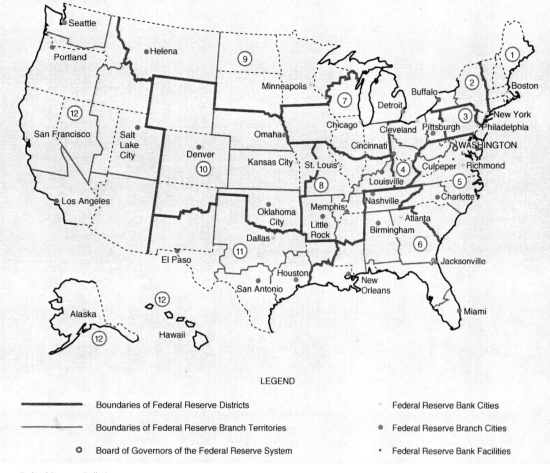

LEGEND

—————— Boundaries of Federal Reserve Districts

——— Boundaries of Federal Reserve Branch Territories

⊙ Board of Governors of the Federal Reserve System

· Federal Reserve Bank Cities

● Federal Reserve Branch Cities

· Federal Reserve Bank Facilities

Source: *Federal Reserve Bulletin*.

One of the seven board members is selected by the president to be Federal Reserve chairman for a four-year term, which may be renewed. The chairman has no more voting power than any other member, but may have more influence. For example, both Paul Volcker, who served as chairman from 1979 to 1987, and Alan Greenspan, who succeeded him in 1987, are regarded as very persuasive.

The board has two main roles: (1) regulating commercial banks and (2) controlling monetary policy. It supervises and regulates commercial banks that are members of the Fed and bank holding companies. It oversees the operation of the 12 Federal Reserve district banks as they provide services to depository institutions and supervise specific commercial banks. It also establishes regulations on consumer finance. Previously, the board was responsible for determining ceiling interest rates on bank deposits, but those ceilings were completely phased out by 1986 as a result of the Depository Institutions Deregulation and Monetary Control Act of 1980. The board continues to participate in the supervision of member banks and in setting credit controls, such as margin requirements (percentage of a purchase of securities that must be paid with nonborrowed funds).

With regard to monetary policy, the board has direct control over two monetary policy tools and participates in the control of a third tool. First, it has the power to revise reserve requirements imposed on depository institutions. Second, it authorizes changes in the **discount rate,** or the interest rate charged on Fed district bank loans to depository institutions. Any changes in the discount rate or reserve requirements can affect the money supply level, as explained later in the chapter. The board can also control the money supply by participating in the decisions of the Federal Open Market Committee, discussed next.

Federal Open Market Committee (FOMC)

http://www.federalreserve .gov Obtain the minutes of the most recent Federal Open Market Committee (FOMC).

The **Federal Open Market Committee (FOMC)** is made up of the seven members of the Board of Governors plus the presidents of five Fed district banks (the New York district bank plus four of the other 11 Fed district banks as determined on a rotating basis). Presidents of the seven remaining Fed district banks typically participate in the FOMC meetings but are not allowed to vote on policy decisions. The chairman of the Board of Governors serves as chairman of the FOMC.

The main goals of the FOMC are to promote high employment, economic growth, and price stability. Achievement of these goals would stabilize financial markets, interest rates, foreign exchange values, and so on. Because the FOMC may not be able to achieve all of its main goals simultaneously, it may concentrate on resolving a particular economic problem.

The FOMC attempts to achieve its goals through control of the money supply. It meets about every six weeks to review economic conditions and determine appropriate monetary policy to improve economic conditions and prevent potential adverse conditions from erupting.

In order to make monetary policy decisions, FOMC members assess the current economic situation, using statistics on recent economic growth, inflation, and the unemployment rate. They also review global economic conditions and their relationship with U.S. conditions. Then, the members discuss their main concerns about the U.S. economy. For example, when the unemployment rate is high and the inflation rate is low, they focus on correcting unemployment by using a stimulative monetary policy. Conversely, when inflation is high and unemployment is low, the focus is on reducing inflation by using a restrictive monetary policy (designed to slow economic growth and thereby reduce inflation). When both the unemployment rate and the inflation rate are high, the FOMC faces a more challenging dilemma, as it is difficult to achieve a monetary policy that can reduce both problems simultaneously.

Advisory Committees

The Federal Advisory Council consists of one member from each Federal Reserve district. Each district's member is elected each year by the board of directors of the respective district bank. The council meets with the Board of Governors in Washington, D.C., at least four times a year and makes recommendations about economic and banking issues.

The Consumer Advisory Council is made up of 30 members, representing the financial institutions industry and its consumers. This committee normally meets with the Board of Governors four times a year to discuss consumer issues.

The Thrift Institutions Advisory Council is made up of 12 members, representing savings banks, savings and loan associations, and credit unions. Its purpose is to offer views on issues specifically related to these institutions. It meets with the Board of Governors three times a year.

Integration of Federal Reserve Components

Exhibit 4.2 shows the relationships among the various components of the Federal Reserve System. The advisory committees advise the board, while the board oversees operations of the district banks. The board and representatives of the district banks make up the FOMC.

Monetary Policy Tools

Changes in the money supply can have a major impact on economic conditions. Financial market participants closely monitor the Fed's actions so that they can anticipate how the money supply will be affected. They then use this information to forecast economic conditions and securities prices. The relationship between the money supply and economic conditions is discussed in detail in the following chapter. First, it is important to understand *how* the Fed controls the money supply.

The Fed can use three monetary policy tools to either increase or decrease the money supply:

- Open market operations
- Adjustments in the discount rate
- Adjustments in the reserve requirement ratio

Open Market Operations

The FOMC meets eight times a year. At each meeting, the target money supply growth level and interest rate level are determined, and actions are taken to implement the monetary policy dictated by the FOMC. If the Fed wants to consider changing the money growth or interest rate targets before its next scheduled meeting because of unusual circumstances, it may engage in a conference call meeting.

FOMC Meeting Agenda About two weeks before the FOMC meeting, FOMC members are sent the **Beige Book,** which is a consolidated report of regional economic conditions in each of the 12 districts. Each Federal Reserve district bank is responsible for reporting its regional conditions, and all of these reports are consolidated to compose the Beige Book.

The FOMC meeting is conducted in the Board room of the building where the Board of Governors is located in Washington, D.C. The meeting is attended by the seven members of the Board of Governors, the 12 presidents of the Fed district banks, and staff members (typically economists) of the Board of Governors. The meeting begins with presentations by the staff members about current economic conditions and recent economic trends. They provide data and trends for wages, consumer prices, unemployment, gross domestic product, business inventories, foreign exchange rates, interest rates, and financial market conditions.

http://www.federalreserve.gov/policy.htm Provides minutes of FOMC meetings. Notice from the minutes how much attention is given to any economic indicators that can be used to anticipate future economic growth or inflation.

EXHIBIT 4.2

Integration of Federal
Reserve Components

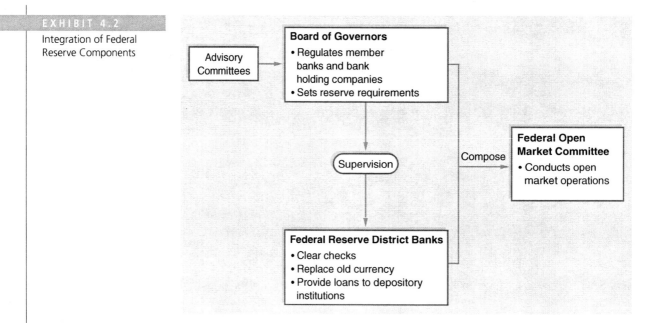

The staff members also assess production levels, business investment, residential construction, international trade, and international economic growth. This assessment is conducted to predict economic growth and inflation in the United States, assuming that the Fed does not adjust its monetary policy. For example, a reduction in business inventories may lead to an expectation of stronger economic growth, as firms will need to boost production in order to replenish inventories. Conversely, an increase in inventories may indicate that firms will reduce their production and possibly their work force as well. An increase in business investment indicates that businesses are expanding their production capacity and are likely to increase their production in the future. An increase in economic growth in foreign countries is important because a portion of the increased incomes in those countries will be spent on U.S. products or services. The Fed uses this information to determine whether U.S. economic growth is adequate.

Much attention is also given to any factors that can affect inflation. For example, oil prices are closely monitored because they affect the cost of producing and transporting many products. A decline in business inventories when production is near full capacity may indicate an excessive demand for products that will pull prices up. This condition indicates higher inflation because firms may raise the prices of their products when they are producing near full capacity and experience shortages. If firms attempt to expand capacity under these conditions, they will have to raise wages to obtain additional qualified employees. They will incur higher costs from raising wages and therefore raise the prices of their products. The Fed becomes concerned when several indicators suggest that higher inflation is likely.

The staff members typically base their forecasts for economic conditions on the assumption that the prevailing monetary growth level will still be applied in the future. When it is highly likely that the monetary growth level will be changed, they provide forecasts for economic conditions under different monetary growth scenarios. Their goal is to provide facts and economic forecasts, but not to make judgments about the appropriate monetary policy. The members normally receive some economic information a few days before the meeting so that they are prepared when listening to the presentations by staff members.

Once the presentations are completed, each FOMC member has a chance to offer recommendations about whether the prevailing monetary growth and interest rate target levels should be changed and, if so, how they should be changed. Even the nonvoting members are given time to offer recommendations. The chairman of the Fed may also offer a recommendation and usually has some influence over the other members. After each member of the FOMC has provided his or her recommendation, the voting members of the FOMC vote on whether the prevailing money supply and interest rate target levels should be revised. Most FOMC decisions on monetary policy are unanimous, although it is not unusual for some decisions to have one or two dissenting votes.

Communication to the Trading Desk If the Fed determines that a change in its monetary policy is appropriate, its decision is forwarded to the **Trading Desk** (or the **Open Market Desk**) at the New York Fed district bank. It is here that open market operations, or the Fed's trading of government securities, are carried out. The FOMC's decision on the target money supply level is forwarded to the Trading Desk at the New York Federal Reserve district bank through a statement called the **policy directive.** The FOMC objectives are specified in the form of a target range, such as an annualized growth rate of 3 to 5 percent in the money supply over the next few months, rather than one specific money supply level.

The FOMC also specifies a desired target range for the federal funds rate, the rate charged by banks on short-term loans to each other. Even though this rate is determined by the banks that participate in the federal funds market, it is subject to the supply and demand for funds in the banking system. Thus, the Fed can influence the federal funds rate by revising the amount of funds in the banking system. In recent years, the Fed has specified a single federal funds target rate when it has engaged in open market operations. Since all short-term interest rates are affected by the supply of and demand for funds, they tend to move together. Thus, the Fed's actions affect all short-term interest rates that are market determined and may even affect long-term interest rates as well.

Role of the Trading Desk After receiving the policy directive from the FOMC, the manager of the Trading Desk instructs traders who work at that desk on the amount of government securities to buy or sell in the secondary market based on the directive. The buying and selling of government securities (through the Trading Desk) is referred to as **open market operations;** this is the most common means by which the Fed controls the money supply. Even though the Trading Desk at the Federal Reserve Bank of New York receives a policy directive from the FOMC only eight times a year, it continuously uses open market operations in response to ongoing changes in bank deposit levels to maintain the money supply within the specified target range.

Fed Purchase of Securities When traders at the Trading Desk at the Federal Reserve Bank of New York are instructed to purchase a specified dollar amount of securities, they call government securities dealers. The dealers provide a list of securities for sale that gives the denomination and maturity of each security as well as the dealer's ask quote (the price at which the dealer is willing to sell the security). From this list, the traders attempt to purchase those that are most attractive (lowest prices for whatever maturities are desired) until they have purchased the amount requested by the manager of the Trading Desk. The accounting department of the New York district bank then notifies the government bond department to receive and pay for those securities.

When the Fed purchases securities through the government securities dealers, the account balances of the dealers are credited with this amount. Thus, the total amount of funds at the dealers' banks increases. The total funds of commercial banks increase by the dollar amount of securities purchased by the Fed. This activity initiated by the Fed's policy directive represents a loosening of money supply growth.

The Trading Desk is sometimes directed to buy a sufficient amount of Treasury securities to force a decline in the federal funds rate to a new targeted level set by the FOMC. The Trading Desk then buys Treasury securities until it has reduced the federal funds rate to the new targeted level. As the supply of funds in the banking system increases, the federal funds rate declines along with other interest rates.

The Fed's purchase of government securities has a different impact than a purchase by another investor would have because the Fed's purchase results in additional bank funds and increases the ability of banks to make loans and create new deposits. An increase in funds can allow for a net increase in deposit balances and therefore an increase in the money supply. Conversely, the purchase of government securities by someone other than the Fed (such as an investor) results in offsetting account balance positions at commercial banks.

Fed Sale of Securities If the Trading Desk at the Federal Reserve Bank of New York is instructed to decrease the money supply, its traders sell government securities (obtained from previous purchases) to government securities dealers. The securities are sold to the dealers that submit the highest bids. As the dealers pay for the securities, their account balances are reduced. Thus, the total amount of funds at commercial banks is reduced by the market value of the securities sold by the Fed. This activity initiated by the FOMC's policy directive is referred to as a tightening of money supply growth.

The Trading Desk is sometimes directed to sell a sufficient amount of Treasury securities to increase the federal funds rate to a new targeted level set by the FOMC. When the Trading Desk sells a sufficient amount of Treasury securities, it creates a shortage of funds in the banking system. Consequently, the federal funds rate increases along with other interest rates.

Fed Use of Repurchase Agreements In some cases, the Fed may desire to increase the aggregate level of bank funds for only a few days to ensure adequate liquidity in the banking system on those days. Under these conditions, the Trading Desk may trade **repurchase agreements** rather than government securities. It purchases Treasury securities from government securities dealers with an agreement to sell back the securities at a specified date in the near future. Initially, the level of funds rises as the securities are sold; it is then reduced when the dealers repurchase the securities. The Trading Desk uses repurchase agreements during holidays and other such periods to correct temporary imbalances in the level of bank funds. To correct a temporary excess of funds, the Trading Desk sells some of its Treasury securities holdings to securities dealers and agrees to repurchase them at a specified future date.

How Open Market Operations Affect Interest Rates Even though most interest rates are market determined, the Fed can have a strong influence on these rates by controlling the supply of loanable funds. When the Fed uses open market operations to increase bank funds, banks have more funds that can be loaned out. This can influence various market-determined interest rates. First, the federal funds rate may decline because some banks have a larger supply of excess funds to lend out in the federal funds market. Second, banks with excess funds may offer new loans at a lower interest rate in order to make use of these funds. Third, these banks may also lower interest rates offered on deposits because they have more than adequate funds to conduct existing operations.

Since open market operations commonly involve the buying or selling of Treasury bills, the yields on Treasury securities are influenced along with the yields (interest rates) offered on bank deposits. For example, when the Fed buys Treasury bills as a means of increasing the money supply, it places upward pressure on their prices. Since these securities offer a fixed value to investors at maturity, a higher price translates into a lower yield for investors who buy them and hold them until maturity. While Treasury yields are affected directly by open market operations, bank rates are also affected because of the change in the money supply that open market operations bring about.

As the yields on Treasury bills and bank deposits decline, investors search for alternative investments such as other debt securities. As more funds are invested in these securities, the yields will decline. Thus, open market operations used to increase bank funds influence not only bank deposit and loan rates but also the yields on other debt securities. The reduction in yields on debt securities lowers the cost of borrowing for the issuers of new debt securities. This can encourage potential borrowers (including corporations and individuals) to borrow and make expenditures that they might not have made if interest rates were higher.

If open market operations are used to reduce bank funds, the opposite effects occur. More banks have deficient funds, and fewer banks have any excess funds. Thus, there is upward pressure on the federal funds rate, on the loan rates charged to individuals and firms, and on the rates offered to bank depositors. As bank deposit rates rise, some investors may be encouraged to create bank deposits rather than invest in other debt securities. This activity reduces the amount of funds available for these debt instruments, thereby increasing the yield offered on the instruments. More specific details about how money supply adjustments can affect interest rates and economic conditions are provided in the following chapter.

Dynamic versus Defensive Open Market Operations Depending on the intent, open market operations can be classified as either **dynamic** or **defensive.** Dynamic operations are implemented to increase or decrease the level of funds; defensive operations offset the impact of other conditions that affect the level of funds. For example, if the Fed expects a large inflow of cash into commercial banks, it could offset this inflow by selling some of its Treasury security holdings.

Open Market Operations in Response to the Crash On October 19, 1987, stock prices declined by more than 22 percent on average, the largest decline in history. The Federal Reserve System took action to prevent further adverse effects. On the morning after the crash, the Fed issued a statement that it was prepared to provide liquidity to the financial markets. It became actively involved in open market operations to ensure adequate liquidity. Because it was concerned that economic growth would be adversely affected by the crash, the Fed loosened the money supply.

The Fed also monitored bank deposit balances to ensure that the crash did not cause runs on bank deposits. It also monitored credit relationships between commercial banks and securities firms, which can change abruptly during a financial crisis. In general, the financial fears that caused the crash did not escalate, and financial markets stabilized shortly after the crash. The Fed's efforts to ensure adequate liquidity and restore confidence in the financial system may have been partially responsible for calming the markets.

Open Market Operations in Response to the Weak U.S. Economy When the U.S. economy weakened in 2001, the Fed attempted to stimulate the economy by using open market operations to increase money supply growth. As a result of these open market operations, the federal funds rate and other short-term interest rates declined. Although the lower rates reduced the cost of borrowing, businesses did not respond to the lower interest rates; that is, they did not decide to borrow just because interest rates were lower. This lack of response led to continued efforts by the Fed to stimulate the economy. During 2001, the Fed made 11 attempts to reduce interest rates. Each effort was associated with an adjustment of either .25 percent or .50 percent in the federal funds target rate. The economy remained weak in 2002, but improved in 2003. The rebound in the economy was partially attributed to the low interest rates.

Open Market Operations in Response to the September 11 Attack on the United States The terrorist attack on September 11, 2001, directly affected the U.S. financial center in New York City. Stock markets were closed for the remainder of the week. The FOMC held a telephone conference call on the day of the attack. It decided to use open market operations so that it could add liquidity to the banking system in case individuals began to withdraw funds from cash machines out of fear of a banking crisis. The FOMC recognized that the attack might slow the economy even further, but decided not to reduce the federal funds target rate at that time.

The stock markets remained closed until September 17. Early on the morning of September 17, the FOMC held another telephone conference call and decided to use open market operations to reduce the federal funds target rate by .50 percent just before the stock markets reopened. Although stocks declined substantially on that day, the effects would likely have been worse if the Fed had not intervened.

Adjusting the Discount Rate

The discount window of the Fed offers loans to depository institutions to correct liquidity problems. The loans are normally for very short-term periods such as one day or a week. Credit extended by the Fed represents an increase in funds at depository institutions. If depository institutions borrow from one another instead, funds are simply transferred among institutions, and the total level of funds is not increased.

To increase the money supply, the Fed (specifically, the Board of Governors) used to authorize a reduction in the discount rate. This encouraged depository institutions that are short on funds to borrow from the Fed rather than from other sources such as the federal funds market. To decrease the money supply, the Fed discouraged use of the discount window by increasing the discount rate. Depository institutions in need of short-term funds obtained funding from alternative sources. As existing discount window loans were repaid to the Fed and new loans were obtained from sources other than the discount window, the level of funds decreased.

In January 2003, the Fed changed the structure of its discount rate. It classified its loans as primary credit or secondary credit. Primary credit may be used for any purpose and is available only to depository institutions that meet specific requirements for financial soundness (such as sufficient capital). Secondary credit is provided to banks that do not qualify for primary credit. A premium above the discount rate is charged for secondary credit. That is, depository institutions that do not meet the requirements for financial soundness pay a higher rate on Fed loans, which reflects a risk premium.

In addition to changing the structure of the discount rate in January 2003, the Fed also established a policy in which the discount rate (now also referred to as the primary credit lending rate) would be set at a level above the federal funds rate. Thus, loans from the Fed should serve only as a backup source of funds for depository institutions.

Before the 2003 policy, adjustments to the discount rate were sometimes viewed as signals about the Fed's future monetary policy. An increase in the discount rate was sometimes interpreted as a signal that the Fed may implement a loose money policy, and reduce the federal funds rate in the near future. Conversely, a reduction in the discount rate was sometimes interpreted as a signal that the Fed may implement a tight money policy, and increase the federal funds rate in the near future. As a result of the 2003 policy, the discount rate is adjusted in response to changes in the federal funds rate. Thus, the discount rate is no longer an effective monetary policy tool, and no longer serves as a possible signal of changes in other interest rates.

Adjusting the Reserve Requirement Ratio

Depository institutions are subject to a **reserve requirement ratio,** which is the proportion of their deposit accounts that must be held as reserves. This ratio is set by the Board of Governors. Depository institutions have historically been forced to maintain between 8 and 12 percent of their transactions accounts (such as checking accounts) and a smaller proportion of their other savings accounts as required reserves, which cannot be used to earn interest.

Because the reserve requirement ratio affects the degree to which the money supply can change, it is sometimes modified by the Board of Governors to adjust the money supply. When the board reduces the reserve requirement ratio, it increases the proportion of a bank's deposits that can be lent out by depository institutions. As the funds loaned out are spent, a portion of them will return to the depository institutions in the form of new deposits. The lower the reserve requirement ratio, the greater the lending capacity of depository institutions, so any initial change in bank reserves can cause a larger change in the money supply.

During the 1980s, the Board of Governors removed the reserve requirement ratio on some types of time deposits. In December 1990, the reserve requirement ratio on negotiable certificates of deposit was removed. In 1992, the reserve requirement ratio on transactions accounts was reduced from 12 percent to 10 percent, where it has remained.

How Reserve Requirement Adjustments Affect Money Growth To illustrate how adjustments in the reserve requirement ratio can affect money supply growth, a simplified example follows. Assume the following information:

Assumption 1. Banks obtain all their funds from demand deposits and use all funds except required reserves to make loans.

Assumption 2. The public does not store any cash; any funds withdrawn from banks are spent; and any funds received are deposited in banks.

Assumption 3. The reserve requirement ratio on demand deposits is 10 percent.

Based on these assumptions, 10 percent of all bank deposits are maintained as required reserves, and the other 90 percent are loaned out (zero excess reserves). Now assume that the Fed initially uses open market operations by purchasing $100 million worth of Treasury securities.

As the Treasury securities dealers sell securities to the Fed, their deposit balances at commercial banks increase by $100 million. Banks maintain 10 percent of the $100 million, or $10 million, as required reserves and lend out the rest. As the $90 million lent out is spent, it returns to banks as new demand deposit accounts (by whoever receives the funds that were spent). Banks maintain 10 percent, or $9 million, of these new deposits as required reserves and lend out the remainder ($81 million). Because of this cycle, the initial increase in demand deposits (money) multiplies into a much larger

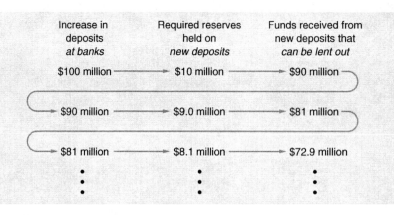

amount. Exhibit 4.3 summarizes this cycle. This cycle will not continue forever. Every time the funds lent out return to a bank, a portion (10 percent) is retained as required reserves. Thus, the amount of new deposits created is less for each round. Under the previous assumptions, the initial money supply injection of $100 million would multiply by 1/(reserve requirement ratio), or 1/.10, to equal 10, so the total change in the money supply once the cycle is complete is $100 million × 10 = $1 billion.

As this simplified example demonstrates, an initial injection of funds will multiply into a larger amount. The reserve requirement controls the amount of loanable funds that can be created from new deposits. A higher reserve requirement ratio causes an initial injection of funds to multiply by a smaller amount. Conversely, a lower reserve requirement ratio causes it to multiply by a greater amount. In this way, the Fed can adjust money supply growth by adjusting the reserve requirement ratio.

Our example exaggerates the amount by which money multiplies. Consumers sometimes hold cash, and banks sometimes hold excess reserves, contradicting the assumptions of banks holding only demand deposits and zero excess reserves. Consequently, major leakages occur, and money does not multiply to the extent shown in the example. The money multiplier can change over time because of changes in the excess reserve level and in consumer preferences for demand deposits versus time deposits (which are not included in the most narrow definition of money). This complicates the task of forecasting how an initial adjustment in bank reserves will ultimately affect the money supply level.

Comparison of Monetary Policy Tools

Exhibit 4.4 compares the ways that monetary policy tools increase or decrease money supply growth. The Fed most frequently uses open market operations as a monetary policy tool because they are convenient and because the other tools have certain disadvantages.

An adjustment in the discount rate affected the money supply only if depository institutions responded (borrow more or less from the Fed than normal) to the adjustment. In addition, borrowings through the discount window are for a very short term, so any adjustment in funds resulting from an increase or decrease in loans from the Fed is only temporary. Now that changes in the discount rate are dictated by changes in the federal funds rate, the discount rate is not a useful monetary policy tool.

An adjustment in the reserve requirement ratio can cause erratic shifts in the money supply. Thus, the probability of missing the target money supply level is higher when using the reserve requirement ratio.

EXHIBIT 4.4 Comparison of Monetary Policy Tools

Monetary Policy Tool	To Increase Money Supply Growth	To Decrease Money Supply Growth
Open market operations	Fed should (through the Trading Desk) purchase government securities in the secondary market.	Fed should (through the Trading Desk) sell government securities in the secondary market.
Adjusting the discount rate	Fed used to lower the discount rate to encourage borrowing through the discount window.	Fed used to raise the discount rate to discourage borrowing through the discount window.
Adjusting reserve requirements	Fed should lower the reserve requirement ratio to cause money to multiply at a higher rate.	Fed should raise the reserve requirement ratio to cause money to multiply at a lower rate.

Open market operations do not suffer from these limitations. In addition, open market operations can be used without signaling the Fed's intentions and can easily be reversed without the public's knowing. A reverse adjustment in the reserve requirement ratio could arouse more concern among the public, reduce the Fed's credibility, and create paranoia in financial markets.

Because the rate by which injected funds will multiply is uncertain (even when leaving the reserve requirement ratio unchanged), there is no guarantee that open market operations will accomplish the money growth target. Even so, they can be used continuously over time to manipulate the money supply toward the desired target.

Impact of Technical Factors on Funds

Even if the Fed does not intervene, the volume of funds can change as a result of so-called technical factors, such as currency in circulation and Federal Reserve float. When the amount of currency in circulation increases (such as during the holiday season), the corresponding increase in net deposit withdrawals reduces funds. When it decreases, the net addition to deposits increases funds. Federal Reserve float is the amount of checks credited to bank funds that have not yet been collected. A rise in float causes an increase in bank funds, and a decrease in float causes a reduction in bank funds.

Staff at the Federal Reserve Bank of New York along with those at the Board of Governors in Washington, D.C., provide daily forecasts of how technical factors such as these will affect the level of funds. The Fed must account for such influences when implementing monetary policy. The manager of the Trading Desk incorporates the expected impact of technical factors on funds into the instructions to traders. If the policy directive calls for growth in funds but technical factors are expected to increase funds, the instructions will call for a smaller injection of funds than if the technical factors did not exist. Conversely, if technical factors are expected to reduce funds, the instructions will call for a larger injection of funds to offset the impact of the technical factors.

Fed Control of the Money Supply

When the Fed manipulates the money supply to influence economic variables, it must decide what form of money to manipulate. The optimal form of money should (1) be controllable by the Fed and (2) have a predictable impact on economic variables when

EXHIBIT 4.5

Comparison of Money
Supply Measures

Money Supply Measures
M1 = currency + checking deposits
M2 = M1 + savings deposits, MMDAs, overnight repurchase agreements, Eurodollars, noninstitutional money market mutual funds, and small time deposits
M3 = M2 + institutional money market mutual funds, large time deposits, and repurchase agreements and Eurodollars lasting more than one day

http://www.federalreserve
.gov/releases Features
various Federal Reserve
statistical releases.

adjusted by the Fed. The most narrow form of money, known as **M1,** includes currency held by the public and checking deposits (such as demand deposits, NOW accounts, and automatic transfer balances) at depository institutions. Although M1 has received the most attention in recent years, it does not include all funds that can be used for transactions purposes. For example, checks can be written against a **money market deposit account (MMDA)** offered by depository institutions or against a money market mutual fund. In addition, funds can easily be withdrawn from savings accounts to make transactions. For this reason, a broader measure of money, called **M2,** also deserves consideration. It includes everything in M1 as well as savings accounts and small time deposits, MMDAs, and some other items. Another measure of money, called **M3,** includes everything in M2 as well as large time deposits and other items. Although there are even a few broader measures of money, M1, M2, and M3 receive the most attention. A comparison of M1, M2, and M3 is provided in Exhibit 4.5.

The Fed first introduced the M1, M2, and M3 monetary aggregates in 1971. In 1978, the Full Employment and Balanced Growth Act (more commonly known as the Humphrey-Hawkins Act) required the Fed to set one-year target ranges for money supply growth twice a year. Particularly during the 1980s, M1 target ranges were closely watched by market participants to anticipate interest rate changes by the Fed.

During the deregulation phase (early 1980s) in the depository institutions industry, various new deposit accounts were created, and households began to switch among accounts. When funds were transferred from demand deposit accounts to MMDAs, M1 was reduced even though the Fed had taken no action to reduce it. When funds were transferred from savings into NOW accounts, M1 increased simply because of a change in household saving habits rather than monetary policy actions. Consequently, the M1 measure became quite volatile over this period and was difficult for the Fed to control. The Fed stopped announcing growth ranges for M1 in 1987.

Since the broader M2 measure includes most deposit accounts, it was not as sensitive to changes in consumer habits. Even though individual components of M2 (such as MMDAs and NOW accounts) were affected by deregulation, the overall level of M2 was not.

The money measurement M1 is more volatile than M2 or M3. Since M1 can change simply because of changes in the types of deposits maintained by households, M2 and M3 are more reliable measures for monitoring and controlling the money supply.

Limitations of Controlling Money Supply

In the 1970s, the Fed attempted to simultaneously control the money supply and interest rates within specified target ranges. It used the federal funds rate as its representative interest rate to control, which in turn can influence other interest rates. Simultaneous control of the money supply and federal funds rate is not always possible. Assume that the Fed sets hypothetical target ranges for money supply growth and the federal funds rate. Assume that both variables are near the upper boundary of their respective ranges. If the Fed desires to maintain the federal funds rate within its range, it would likely inject more funds into the economy (increase money supply growth). However, this will force the money supply growth above its upper boundary. If instead the Fed maintains money supply growth within its range, it may be unable to prevent the federal funds rate from rising above its upper boundary.

The Fed recognized that it could not simultaneously control both variables and as of October 1979 chose to focus primarily on the money supply. Over the next decades, the Fed hit its long-term money supply targets with some success. From time to time, however, various factors distorted the relationship between the money supply and economic conditions.

In the early 1990s, when interest rates were at a low point, many savers moved funds out of savings accounts and time deposits into stock and bond mutual funds, which are not included in any of the money supply measures. Consequently, in July 1993, Alan Greenspan announced in congressional testimony that the measures of money are not always reliable indicators of financial conditions in the economy.

For the next several years, the Fed focused on maintaining the federal funds rate within a narrow target range. When the Humphrey-Hawkins legislation requiring the Fed to set target ranges for money supply growth expired in 2000, the Fed announced that it would no longer set such targets. Nevertheless, the Fed also stated that the behavior of money and credit would continue to have value for gauging economic and financial conditions. In addition, M2 still remains a component of the Index of Leading Economic Indicators.

Monetary Control Act of 1980

In 1980 Congress passed the **Depository Institutions Deregulation and Monetary Control Act (DIDMCA).** Commonly referred to as the Monetary Control Act, it had two key objectives. First, it was intended to deregulate some aspects of the depository institutions industry (discussed in the chapters on depository institutions). Second, it was intended to enhance the Fed's ability to control the money supply.

Before DIDMCA, member banks of the Federal Reserve were subject to its reserve requirements, and nonmember banks were subject to the reserve requirements of their respective states. Nonmember banks often had an advantage in that they could typically maintain their required reserves in some interest-bearing form (such as Treasury securities). A member bank's required reserves could be held only as balances at the Fed or as vault cash and therefore could not earn interest. This disadvantage to member banks became more pronounced in the 1970s, when interest rates were generally higher than in previous years. The opportunity cost of tying up funds in a non-interest-bearing form increased. As a result, some member banks dropped their membership.

As Fed memberships decreased, so did the Fed's ability to control the money supply through reserve requirement adjustments, because it could adjust reserve requirements only of *member* banks. The Monetary Control Act mandates that all depository institutions be subject to the same reserve requirements imposed by the Fed. The reserve requirements were reduced relative to what the Fed previously required, but all required reserves were still to be held in a non-interest-bearing form. The revised reserve requirements were phased in over an eight-year period.

A related provision of the Monetary Control Act is that all depository institutions must report their deposit levels promptly to the Fed. This improves the Fed's knowledge of the current level of deposits in the banking system at any point in time. In the past, the Fed may have underestimated the prevailing money supply at times and thus increased the money supply above the level desired. With the improved reporting system, it has a better feel for the prevailing money supply level and therefore makes better adjustments.

In addition to its reserve requirement and reporting provisions, the Monetary Control Act allowed all depository institutions that offer transaction accounts (such as demand deposits or NOW accounts) to have access to the discount window. Previously, only member banks were allowed access. This provision provided the Fed additional control over the money supply because more institutions have access to the discount window. As noted earlier, however, the Fed no longer uses discount rate adjustments to control the money supply.

Global Monetary Policy

GL ⊕ BAL **ASPECTS**

Each country has its own central bank that conducts monetary policy. The central banks of industrialized countries tend to have somewhat similar goals, which essentially reflect price stability (low inflation) and economic growth (low unemployment). Resources and conditions vary among countries, however, so a given central bank may focus more on a particular economic goal.

Like the Fed, central banks of other industrialized countries use open market operations, reserve requirement adjustments, and adjustments in the interest rate they charge on loans to banks as monetary policy tools. The monetary policy tools are generally used as a means of affecting local market interest rates in order to influence economic conditions.

Because country economies are integrated, the Fed must consider economic conditions in other major countries when assessing the U.S. economy. The Fed may be most effective when it coordinates its activities with those of central banks of other countries. Central banks commonly work together when they intervene in the foreign exchange market, but coordinating monetary policies can be difficult because of conflicts of interest.

A Single Eurozone Monetary Policy

http://www.federalreserve
.gov Provides links on the
European Central Bank and
other foreign central banks.

The national currencies of the following 12 European countries were recently withdrawn from the financial system and replaced by the euro: Austria, Belgium, Finland, France, Germany, Greece, Ireland, Italy, Luxembourg, the Netherlands, Portugal, and Spain. The three other members of the European Union (Denmark, Sweden, United Kingdom) at that time decided not to participate in the euro initially but may join later. In 2004, 10 emerging countries in Europe, including the Czech Republic and Hungary, joined the European Union and may participate in the euro later if they satisfy the limitations imposed on government deficits.

The European Central Bank (ECB), based in Frankfurt, is responsible for setting monetary policy for all participating European countries. Its objective is to control inflation in the participating countries and to stabilize (within reasonable boundaries) the value of the euro with respect to other major currencies. Thus, the ECB's monetary goals of price stability and currency stability are somewhat similar to those of individual countries around the world, but differ in that they are focused on a group of countries rather than a single country. Because participating countries are subject to the monetary policy imposed by the ECB, a given country will no longer have full control over the monetary policy imposed within its borders at any given time. The implementation of a common monetary policy may lead to more political unification among participating countries and encourage them to develop similar national defense and foreign policies.

Impact of the Euro on Monetary Policy As just described, the use of a common currency forces countries to abide by a common monetary policy. Any changes in the money supply affect all European countries using the euro as their form of money. Having a single currency also means that the interest rate offered on government securities must be similar across the participating European countries. Any discrepancy in rates would encourage investors within these countries to invest in the country with the highest rate, which would realign the interest rates among the countries.

Although having a single monetary policy may allow for more consistent economic conditions across the eurozone countries, it prevents any participating country from solving local economic problems with its own unique monetary policy. Eurozone governments may disagree on the ideal monetary policy to enhance their local economies, but they must agree on a single monetary policy. Yet any given policy used in a particular period may enhance some countries and adversely affect others. Each participating country is still able to apply its own fiscal policy (tax and government expenditure decisions), however.

One concern about the euro is that each of the participating countries has its own agenda, which may prevent unified decisions about the future direction of the eurozone economies. Each country was supposed to show restraint on fiscal policy spending so that it could improve its budget deficit situation. Nevertheless, some countries have ignored restraint in favor of resolving domestic unemployment problems. The euro's initial instability was partially attributed to political maneuvering as individual countries tried to serve their own interests at the expense of the other participating countries. This lack of solidarity is exactly the reason why there was some concern about using a single currency (and therefore monetary policy) among several European countries.

Variations in the Value of the Euro Since the euro was introduced in 1999, it has experienced a bumpy ride. Its value initially declined substantially against the British pound, the dollar, and many other currencies. By October 2001, its value was $.90, or about 25 percent less than its value when it was introduced. The weakness was partially attributed to capital outflows from Europe. More money was flowing out of Europe and into U.S. and other financial markets than was flowing from these countries to Europe. The net outflows from Europe were partially caused by lack of confidence in the euro. Investors preferred to hold assets denominated in dollars than in euros.

During the 2002–2003 period, however, the euro appreciated substantially. One reason for its strength in this period was that the interest rate on the euro was higher than that of the dollar. Thus, capital flowed to the eurozone to take advantage of the higher interest rate on euro-denominated debt securities.

Global Central Bank Coordination

In some cases, the central banks of various countries coordinate their efforts for a common cause. Shortly after the terrorist attack on the United States on September 11, 2001, central banks of several countries injected money denominated in their respective currencies into the banking system to provide more liquidity. This strategy was intended to ensure that sufficient money would be available in case customers began to withdraw funds from banks or cash machines. On September 17, 2001, the Fed's move to reduce interest rates before the U.S. stock market reopened was immediately followed by similar decisions by the Bank of Canada (Canada's central bank) and the European Central Bank.

Sometimes, however, central banks have conflicting objectives. For example, it is not unusual for two countries to simultaneously experience weak economies. In this situation, each central bank may consider intervening to weaken its home currency, which could increase foreign demand for exports denominated in that currency. If both central banks attempt this type of intervention simultaneously, however, the exchange rate between the two currencies will be subject to conflicting forces.

ILLUSTRATION Today, the Fed plans to intervene directly in the foreign exchange market by selling dollars for yen in an attempt to weaken the dollar. Meanwhile, the Bank of Japan plans to sell yen for dollars in the foreign exchange market in an attempt to weaken the yen. The effects are offsetting. One central bank can attempt to have a more powerful impact by selling more of its home currency in the foreign exchange market, but the other central bank may respond to offset that force.

SUMMARY

- The key components of the Federal Reserve System are the Board of Governors and the Federal Open Market Committee. The Board of Governors determines the reserve requirements on account balances at depository institutions. It also represents an important subset of the Federal Open Market Committee (FOMC), which determines the monetary policy of the United States. The FOMC's monetary policy has a major influence on interest rates and other economic conditions.

- The three main tools used by the Fed to conduct monetary policy are open market operations, the discount rate, and the reserve requirement ratio. In its open market operations, the Fed buys and sells securities as a means of adjusting the money supply. The Fed purchases securities as a means of increasing the money supply and sells them as a means of reducing the money supply.

   The Fed used to raise the discount rate as a restrictive monetary policy to discourage bank borrowing from the Fed. Conversely, the Fed used to reduce the discount rate as an expansionary policy to encourage more bank borrowing from the Fed.

   The Fed can raise the reserve requirement ratio as a restrictive monetary policy to reduce the degree to which money multiplies. Conversely, the Fed can reduce the ratio as an expansionary monetary policy to increase the degree to which money multiplies.

- In 1980, Congress passed DIDMCA, which imposed uniform reserve requirements across all depository institutions. Thus, the reserve requirement became a more powerful monetary policy tool because it affected more depository institutions. DIDMCA also allowed all depository institutions with transaction accounts access to the discount window. However, the discount rate is no longer an effective monetary policy tool.

- Each country has its own central bank, which is responsible for conducting monetary policy to achieve economic goals such as low inflation and low unemployment. Twelve countries in Europe recently adopted a single currency, which causes all of these countries to be subject to the same monetary policy.

Should There Be One Global Central Bank?

Point Yes. One global central bank could serve all countries in the manner that the European Central Bank now serves several European countries. If there was a single central bank, there could be a single monetary policy across all countries.

Counter-Point No. A global central bank could create a global monetary policy only if a single currency was used throughout the world. Moreover, all countries would not agree on the monetary policy that is appropriate.

Who Is Correct? Use InfoTrac or some other source search engine to learn more about this issue. Offer your own opinion on this issue.

1. **The Fed** Briefly describe the origin of the Federal Reserve System. Describe the functions of the Fed district banks.

2. **FOMC** What are the main goals of the Federal Open Market Committee? How does it attempt to achieve these goals?

3. **Open Market Operations** Explain how the Fed increases the money supply through open market operations.

4. **Policy Directive** What is the policy directive, and who carries it out?

5. **Discount Window** How is the money supply adjusted through the discount window? What policy change occurred in 2003 that caused the discount rate to be an ineffective monetary policy tool?

6. **Reserve Requirements** How is money supply growth affected by an increase in the reserve requirement ratio?

7. **Control of Money Supply** Describe the characteristics that would be desirable for a measure of money to be manipulated by the Fed. Explain why it is difficult to simultaneously control the money supply and the federal funds rate.

8. **Monetary Control Act** What are the two key objectives of the Monetary Control Act? How does the Monetary Control Act help the Fed avoid improper adjustments in the money supply?

9. **Impact of Monetary Control Act** Have the reserve requirement provisions of the Monetary Control Act improved the Fed's ability to manipulate the money supply? Explain.

10. **Tools Used by the Fed** Which tool used by the Fed is the most important on a weekly basis from the perspective of financial market participants?

Interpret the following statements made by Wall Street analysts and portfolio managers:

a. "The Fed's future monetary policy will be dependent on the economic indicators to be reported this week."

b. "The Fed's role is to take the punch bowl away just as the party is coming alive."

c. "Inflation will likely increase because real short-term interest rates currently are negative."

Assess the current structure of the Federal Reserve System, using the website http://www.federalreserve.gov.

Who is the current chairman of the Board of Governors? Who is the current vice chairman? Who are the other members of the Board of Governors? How often does the Board meet? When is the next scheduled meeting, and what items are scheduled to be discussed at this meeting?

Anticipating the Fed's Actions As a manager of a large U.S. firm, one of your assignments is to monitor U.S. economic conditions so that you can forecast the demand for products sold by your firm. You recognize that the Federal Reserve attempts to implement monetary policy to affect economic growth and inflation. In addition, you recognize that the federal government implements spending and tax policies (fiscal policy) to affect economic growth and inflation. Yet, it is difficult to achieve high economic growth without igniting inflation. It is often said that the Federal Reserve is independent of the administration in Washington, D.C., yet there is much interaction between monetary and fiscal policies.

Assume that the economy is currently stagnant, and some economists are concerned about the possibility of a recession. Some industries, however, are experiencing high growth, and inflation is higher this year than in the previous five years. Assume that the Federal Reserve chairman's term will expire in four months and that the president of the United States will have to appoint a new chairman (or reappoint the existing chairman). It is widely known that the existing chairman would like to be reappointed. Also assume that next year is an election year for the administration.

a. Given the circumstances, do you expect that the administration will be more concerned about increasing economic growth or reducing inflation?

b. Given the circumstances, do you expect that the Fed will be more concerned about increasing economic growth or reducing inflation?

c. Your firm is relying on you for some insight on how the government will influence economic conditions and therefore the demand for your firm's products. Given the circumstances, what is your forecast of how the government will affect economic conditions?

FLOW OF FUNDS EXERCISE

Monitoring the Fed

Recall that Carson Company has obtained substantial loans from finance companies and commercial banks. The interest rate on the loans is tied to market interest rates and is adjusted every six months. Because of its expectations of a strong U.S. economy, Carson plans to grow in the future by expanding its business and through acquisitions. It expects that it will need substantial long-term financing and plans to borrow additional funds either through loans or by issuing bonds. It is also considering the issuance of stock to raise funds in the next year.

Given its large exposure to interest rates charged on its debt, Carson closely monitors Fed actions. It subscribes to a special service that attempts to monitor the Fed's actions in the Treasury security markets. It recently received an alert from the service that suggested the Fed has been selling large holdings of its Treasury securities in the secondary Treasury securities market.

a. How should Carson interpret the actions by the Fed? That is, will these actions place upward or downward pressure on Treasury securities prices? Explain.

b. Will these actions place upward or downward pressure on Treasury yields? Explain.

c. Will these actions place upward or downward pressure on interest rates? Explain.

WSJ EXERCISE

Reviewing Fed Policies

Review the "Credit Markets" section in recent issues of *The Wall Street Journal* and search for any comments that relate to the Fed's money supply targets or the federal funds target rate. Does it appear that the Fed may attempt to revise its money supply growth target or its federal funds target rate? If so, why?

3

Monetary Theory and Policy

he previous chapter discussed the Fed and how it controls the money supply, information essential to financial market participants. It is just as important for participants to know how changes in the money supply affect the economy, which is the subject of this chapter.

The specific objectives of this chapter are to:

- describe the well-known theories about monetary policy,
- explain the tradeoffs involved in monetary policy,
- describe how financial market participants monitor and forecast the Fed's policies, and
- explain how monetary and fiscal policies are related.

Monetary Theory

The type of monetary policy implemented by the Fed depends on the economic philosophies of the FOMC members. Some of the more well-known theories that can influence the Fed's policies are described here.

Pure Keynesian Theory

One of the most popular theories that can influence Fed policy is the **Keynesian theory,** which was developed by John Maynard Keynes, a British economist. To do justice to this theory would require an entire text. The Keynesian theory suggests how the Fed can affect the interaction between the demand for money and the supply of money to influence interest rates, the aggregate level of spending, and therefore economic growth.

The general points of Keynesian theory can be explained by using the loanable funds framework described in Chapter 2. Recall that the interaction of the supply of loanable funds available and the demand for loanable funds determines the interest rate charged on loanable funds. Much of the demand for loanable funds is by households, corporations, and government agencies that need to borrow money. Recall that the demand schedule indicates the quantity of funds that would be demanded (at that time) at various possible interest rates. This schedule is downward sloping because many potential borrowers would borrow a larger quantity of funds at lower interest rates.

The supply schedule of loanable funds indicates the quantity of funds that would be supplied (at that time) at various possible interest rates. This schedule is upward sloping because suppliers of funds tend to supply a larger amount of funds when the interest rate is higher. Assume that as of today, the demand and supply schedules for loan-

EXHIBIT 5.1 Keynesian View on the Effects of an Increased Money Supply

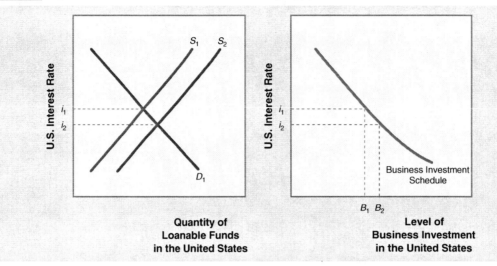

able funds are represented by D_1 and S_1 in the left graph of Exhibit 5.1. Based on these schedules, the equilibrium interest rate would be i_1. The right graph of Exhibit 5.1 represents the typical relationship between the interest rate on loanable funds and the level of business investment as of today. The relation is inverse because corporations are more willing to expand when interest rates are relatively low. Given today's equilibrium interest rate of i_1, the level of business investment is B_1.

Correcting a Weak Economy If the economy is weak, the Fed can increase the level of spending as a means of stimulating the economy. It uses open market operations to increase the money supply, a move that is intended to reduce interest rates and encourage more borrowing and spending.

ILLUSTRATION
The Fed can attempt to stimulate the economy by purchasing Treasury securities in the secondary market. As the investors who sell their Treasury securities receive payment from the Fed, their account balances at financial institutions increase, without any offsetting decrease in the account balances of any other financial institutions. Thus, there is a net increase in the supply of loanable funds. If the Fed's action results in an increase of $5 billion in loanable funds, the quantity of loanable funds supplied will now be $5 billion higher at any possible interest rate level. This means that the supply schedule for loanable funds shifts outward to S_2 in Exhibit 5.1. The difference between S_2 and S_1 is that S_2 incorporates the $5 billion of loanable funds added as a result of the Fed's actions.

Given the shift in the supply schedule for loanable funds, the quantity of loanable funds supplied exceeds the quantity of loanable funds demanded at the interest rate level i_1. Thus, the interest rate will decline to i_2, the level at which the quantities of loanable funds supplied and demanded are equal.

The lower interest rate level causes an increase in the level of business investment from B_1 to B_2. The increase in business investment represents new business spending that was triggered by lower interest rates, which reduced the corporate cost of financing new projects.

The Keynesian philosophy advocates an active role for the federal government in correcting economic problems. The theory conflicts with the classical theory that production (supply) creates its own demand and gained support during the Great Depression when the existing level of production had clearly exceeded demand, causing massive layoffs. Under such conditions, the Keynesian theory would have prescribed stimulative federal government policies, such as high monetary growth.

Correcting High Inflation If excessive inflation is the main concern, the pure Keynesian philosophy would still focus on aggregate spending as the variable that must be adjusted. The Fed can use open market operations to reduce money supply growth, a move that can reduce the level of spending, thereby slowing economic growth and reducing inflationary pressure. A portion of the high inflation is possibly due to excessive spending that is pulling up prices, commonly referred to as **demand-pull inflation.**

ILLUSTRATION The Fed can slow economic growth by selling some of its holdings of Treasury securities in the secondary market. As investors make payments to purchase these Treasury securities, their account balances decrease, without any offsetting increase in the account balances of any other financial institutions. Thus, there is a net decrease in deposit accounts (money), which results in a net decrease in the quantity of loanable funds. Assume that the Fed's action causes a decrease of $5 billion in loanable funds. The quantity of loanable funds supplied will now be $5 billion lower at any possible interest rate level. This reflects an inward shift in the supply schedule from S_1 to S_2, as shown in Exhibit 5.2.

Given the inward shift in the supply schedule for loanable funds, the quantity of loanable funds demanded exceeds the quantity of loanable funds supplied at the original interest rate level (i_1). Thus, the interest rate will increase to i_2, the level at which the quantities of loanable funds supplied and demanded are equal.

The higher interest rate level increases the corporate cost of financing new projects and therefore causes a decrease in the level of business investment from B_1 to B_2. As economic growth is slowed by the reduction in business investment, inflationary pressure may be reduced. Thus, reducing the money supply is an indirect means by which the Fed may reduce inflation.

Summary of Keynesian View Exhibit 5.3 summarizes the Keynesian view of how the Fed (as the central bank of the United States) can affect economic conditions through its

EXHIBIT 5-2 Keynesian View of the Effects of a Reduced Money Supply

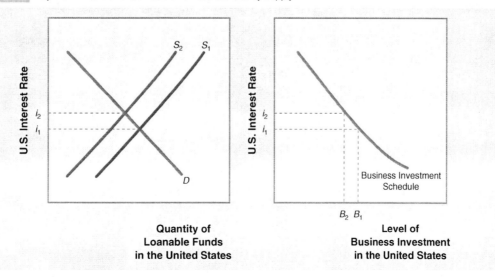

Summary of the Keynesian View of How Monetary Policy Affects Economic Conditions

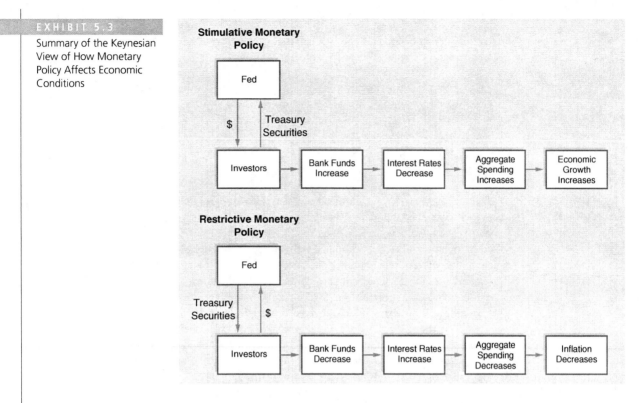

influence on the level of bank funds. The top part of the exhibit illustrates a stimulative monetary policy intended to boost economic growth, and the bottom part illustrates a restrictive monetary policy intended to reduce inflation.

Effects of a Credit Crunch on a Stimulative Policy

The economic impact of monetary policy (as explained by the Keynesian view) may depend on the willingness of banks to lend funds. Even if the Fed increases the level of bank funds during a weak economy, banks may be unwilling to extend credit to some potential borrowers, and the result is a *credit crunch*. It could be argued that if banks do not lend out the newly created funds, the economy will not be stimulated. Yet the perception that banks will not lend out sufficient funds is caused by the effects of a weak economy on loan repayment probability. Banks provide loans only after confirming that the borrower's future cash flows will be adequate to make loan repayments. In a weak economy, the future cash flows of many potential borrowers are more uncertain, causing a reduction in loan applications (demand for loans) and in the number of qualified loan applicants.

Banks and other lending institutions have a responsibility to their depositors, shareholders, and regulators to avoid loans that are likely to default. Because default risk rises during a weak economy, some potential borrowers will be unable to obtain loans. Others may qualify only if they pay high-risk premiums to cover their default risk. Thus, it is possible that the effects of monetary policy can be limited if potential borrowers do not qualify or are unwilling to incur the high-risk premiums. Nevertheless, the credit crunch should not affect borrowers with very low risk. A stimulative monetary policy will be more effective if there are sufficient qualified borrowers that will borrow more funds once interest rates are reduced.

A credit crunch could even occur during a period when a restrictive monetary policy is implemented. As the money supply is reduced, and interest rates rise, some potential borrowers may be unable to obtain loans because the interest payments would be too high. Thus, the effects of the restrictive monetary policy are magnified because the higher interest rates not only discourage some potential borrowers but also prevent others from obtaining loans.

Overall, a credit crunch may partially offset the desired effects of a stimulative monetary policy and magnify the effects of a restrictive monetary policy. Yet, assuming the Fed recognizes the possible influence of the credit crunch, it could modify its specific money supply targets to offset any distortions caused by the crunch.

Quantity Theory and the Monetarist Approach

The quantity theory is applicable to monetary policy because it suggests a particular relationship between the money supply and the degree of economic activity. It is based on the so-called equation of exchange, as follows:

$$MV = P_G Q$$

where M = amount of money in the economy

V = velocity of money

P_G = weighted price level of goods and services in the economy

Q = quantity of goods and services sold

Velocity is the average number of times each dollar changes hands per year. The right side of the equation of exchange represents the total value of goods and services produced. If velocity is constant, a given adjustment in the money supply will produce a predictable change in the total value of goods and services. Thus, a direct relationship between money supply and gross domestic product is evident.

An early form of the theory assumed Q is constant in the short run, which would imply a direct relationship between the money supply and prices. If the money supply is increased, the average price level will increase. However, the assumption of a stable quantity is not realistic today. The original quantity theory has been revised by the **Monetarists** into what is referred to as the **modern quantity theory of money.** Milton Friedman and others relaxed the stable-quantity assumption to suggest that a given increase in the money supply leads to a predictable increase in the value of goods and services produced.

Because velocity represents the ratio of money stock to nominal output, it is affected by any factor that influences this ratio. Income patterns can affect velocity because they influence the amount of money held by households. Factors that increase the ratio of households' money holdings to income reduce velocity, while factors that reduce this ratio increase velocity. Households maintain more money if they receive their income less frequently, whereas credit cards can reduce the need to hold money balances. Expectations of high inflation encourage households to hold smaller money balances, thereby increasing velocity. Nevertheless, Friedman has found that velocity changes in a predictable manner and is not related to fluctuations in the money supply. Therefore, the equation of exchange can be applied to assess how money can affect aggregate spending.

Comparison of the Monetarist and Keynesian Theories The Monetarist approach advocates stable, low growth in the money supply. It may be criticized for being too passive, but its supporters contend that it allows economic problems to resolve themselves without causing additional problems. Suppose the United States experiences a recession. Whereas the typical Keynesian monetary policy prescription would be high money growth, Monetarists would avoid a loose money policy on the grounds that it tends to ignite inflationary expectations, which can increase the demand for money and place upward pressure on interest rates. The Monetarist cure for the recession would not call for any revision in the existing monetary policy. Instead, Monetarists would expect the stagnant economy to reduce corporate and household borrowing and thus result in lower interest rates. Once interest rates are reduced to a low enough level, they will encourage borrowing and therefore stimulate economic growth. Because the Monetarist approach to achieve lower interest rates does not require an increase in money supply growth, inflationary expectations should not be ignited as they might be under the Keynesian approach.

A major limitation of the Monetarist approach is the time required to improve the economy. Is the public willing to suffer while the recession cures itself, or would it prefer a more active (Keynesian) approach to quickly resolve the recession, even though other economic problems might arise as a result?

While recognizing the strong impact of money supply fluctuations on the economy, Monetarists do not believe money growth should be actively adjusted. Instead, they believe in accepting a natural rate of unemployment, and they criticize the government for trying to achieve a rate lower than the natural rate at the price of inflation, especially because the lower rate is unlikely to prevail in the long run. Friedman has found that the impact of money supply growth on economic growth has a long lag time and is uncertain, which is why he advocates a constant rate of monetary growth.

Keynesians and Monetarists also differ in the relative importance they assign to inflation and unemployment. Keynesians tend to focus on maintaining low unemployment and are therefore more willing to tolerate any inflation that results from stimulative monetary policies. Monetarists are more concerned about maintaining low inflation and are therefore more willing to tolerate what they refer to as a natural rate of unemployment.

Theory of Rational Expectations

The **theory of rational expectations** holds that the public accounts for all existing information when forming its expectations. As applied to monetary policy, this theory suggests that households and business, having witnessed historical effects of monetary policy actions, will use this information to forecast the impact of an existing policy and act accordingly.

If the Fed uses a loose monetary policy to stimulate the economy, households will respond by increasing their spending as they anticipate that higher inflation will result from the policy. In addition, businesses will increase their investment in machinery and equipment in an attempt to beat impending higher costs of borrowing. Further, participants in the labor market will negotiate for higher wages to compensate for higher anticipated inflation, and the level of savings will be reduced while the level of borrowing will increase. These forces will offset the impact of an increase in the money supply. Therefore, the policy will not affect interest rates or economic growth. In general, the rational expectations theory supports the contention of Friedman and some other Monetarists that changes in monetary policy are unlikely to have any sustained positive impact on the economy.

ILLUSTRATION   Exhibit 5.4 illustrates the criticism of the Keynesian theory by the Monetarist approach and rational expectations theory. The D_1, S_1, and S_2 curves reflect the Keynesian view on how a stimulative monetary policy (increased money supply) can place downward pressure on interest rates. In fact, these curves are the same as those shown in Exhibit 5.1. A key criticism of the Keynesian view is that it assumes that the quantity of loanable funds demanded is not changed by the adjustment in the money supply. Proponents of the Monetarist approach and rational expectations theory suggest that the

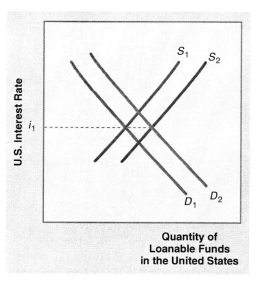

EXHIBIT 5.4

Effects of an Increased Money Supply According to the Monetarist Approach and the Rational Expectations Theory

Quantity of
Loanable Funds
in the United States

increased money supply will increase inflationary expectations, which will cause a higher demand for loanable funds at any possible interest rate. This is reflected by an outward shift in the demand schedule for loanable funds, as illustrated by the D_2 curve in Exhibit 5.4. The outward shift in the demand schedule can completely offset the outward shift in the supply schedule, so the interest rate is not reduced at all. Thus, the level of business investment will not be affected by the Fed's adjustment in the money supply, and the general level of spending in the economy will remain as it was. Under these conditions, the adjustment in the money supply is not effective at stimulating economic growth.

Which Theory Is Correct?

Most economists who serve on the Federal Open Market Committee (FOMC) recognize the virtues and the limitations of each theory. They tend to believe that monetary policy can be an effective tool for controlling economic growth, inflation, and unemployment. Therefore, they adjust monetary growth targets when they see fit, in line with the Keynesian philosophy. However, they are aware of the potential adverse consequence of excessive money supply growth (as suggested by Monetarists), especially when the prevailing inflation level is high. If a stimulative boost in the economy is needed and if severe inflation does not appear to be a potential consequence, a loose-money policy may be implemented. If inflation is a major concern, the Fed is more concerned about the potential adverse effects on inflation that could result from a loose-money policy.

The decisions by the FOMC members may also be influenced by the political party of the president who appointed them. It is important for financial market participants to keep track of the FOMC members over time. As they are replaced, the overall philosophy of the FOMC may shift, resulting in a different monetary policy.

Tradeoff Faced by the Fed

The Fed monitors economic variables, such as inflation, unemployment, and gross domestic product (GDP), over time. Although it does not have direct control over these variables, it can attempt to influence them by manipulating the money supply.

Ideally, the Fed would like to maintain low inflation, steady GDP growth, and low unemployment. Because GDP growth can lead to low unemployment, these two goals may be achieved simultaneously. Consistently maintaining both low inflation and low unemployment is more difficult. For more than 200 years, economists have recognized a possible tradeoff between the two. In 1958, in an article that became famous, Professor A. W. Phillips compared the annual percentage change in the average unemployment rate and wages in the United Kingdom from 1861 to 1913. His research confirmed a negative relationship between the two variables. This relationship suggested that government policies designed to cure unemployment may place upward pressure on wages. In addition, government policies designed to cure inflation may cause more unemployment. This negative relationship came to be known as the **Phillips curve.** The concept provided a new framework for the central bank and the administration to use in determining government policies.

When economists applied the Phillips curve concept to U.S. inflation and unemployment data, they found that the relationship frequently changed. Shifts in the Phillips curve were attributed to unionization, changing productivity, and, more recently, changing expectations about inflation.

When inflation is higher than the Fed deems acceptable, the Fed may consider implementing a tight-money policy to reduce economic growth. As economic growth slows, producers cannot as easily raise their prices and still maintain sales volume. Similarly, workers are not in demand and do not have much bargaining power on wages. Thus, the use of tight money to slow economic growth can reduce the inflation rate. A possible cost of the lower inflation rate is higher unemployment. If the economy becomes stagnant because of the tight-money policy, sales decrease, inventories accumulate, and firms may reduce their workforce to reduce production.

Given that a loose-money policy can reduce unemployment whereas a tight-money policy can reduce inflation, the Fed must determine whether unemployment or inflation is the more serious problem. It may not be able to cure both problems simultaneously. In fact, it may not be able to fully eliminate either problem. Although a loose-money policy can stimulate the economy, it does not guarantee that unskilled workers will be hired. Although a tight-money policy can reduce inflation caused by excessive spending, it cannot reduce inflation caused by such factors as an agreement by the members of the oil cartel to keep oil prices high.

Impact of Other Forces on the Tradeoff

Other forces may also affect the tradeoff faced by the Fed. Consider a situation where because of specific cost factors (higher energy and insurance costs, etc.), inflation will be at least 3 percent. This amount of inflation will exist no matter what type of monetary policy the Fed implements. Also assume that because of the number of unskilled workers and people between jobs, the unemployment rate will be at least 4 percent. A loose-money policy sufficiently stimulates the economy to maintain unemployment at that minimum level of 4 percent. However, such a stimulative policy may also cause additional inflation beyond the 3 percent level. A tight-money policy could maintain inflation at the 3 percent minimum, but unemployment would likely rise above the 4 percent minimum.

This tradeoff is illustrated in Exhibit 5.5. Here the Fed can use a very stimulative (loose-money) policy that is expected to result in Point A (9 percent inflation and 4 percent unemployment). Alternatively, it can use a very restrictive (tight-money) policy that is expected to result in Point B (3 percent inflation and 8 percent unemployment). Or it

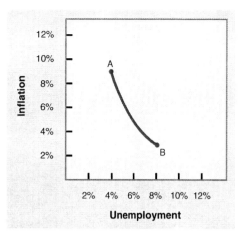

EXHIBIT 5.5

Tradeoff between Reducing Inflation and
Unemployment

can implement a compromise policy that will result in some point along the curve between A and B.

Historical data on annual inflation and unemployment rates show that when one of
these problems worsens, the other does not automatically improve. Both variables can
rise or fall over time. Yet this does not refute the tradeoff faced by the Fed. It simply
means that some outside factors have affected inflation or unemployment or both.

ILLUSTRATION
Recall that the Fed could have achieved Point A, Point B, or somewhere along the
curve connecting these points during a particular time period. Now assume that oil
prices have substantially increased and several product liability lawsuits have occurred.
These events will affect consumer prices such that the minimum inflation rate will be,
say, 6 percent. In addition, assume that various training centers for unskilled workers
have been closed, leaving a higher number of unskilled workers. This forces the minimum unemployment rate to 6 percent. Now the Fed's tradeoff position has changed. The
Fed's new set of possibilities is shown as Curve CD in Exhibit 5.6. Note that the points
reflected on Curve CD are not as desirable as the points along Curve AB that were previously attainable. No matter what type of monetary policy the Fed uses, both the inflation rate and the unemployment rate will be higher than in the previous time period. This is not the fault of the Fed. In fact, the Fed is still faced with a tradeoff between

EXHIBIT 5.6

Adjustment in the Tradeoff between
Unemployment and Inflation over Time

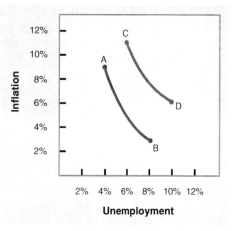

Point C (11 percent inflation, 6 percent unemployment), Point D (6 percent inflation, 10 percent unemployment), or somewhere within those points along Curve CD.

When FOMC members are primarily concerned with either inflation or unemployment, they tend to agree on the type of monetary policy that should be implemented. When both inflation and unemployment are relatively high, however, there is more disagreement among the members about the proper monetary policy to implement. All members would agree that a loose-money policy may stimulate the economy and reduce unemployment, at least in the short run, but would also agree that this policy could ignite inflation. Therefore, some members would likely argue for a tight-money policy to prevent inflation from rising, while other members would suggest that a loose-money policy should be implemented to reduce unemployment even if it results in higher inflation.

How the Fed's Focus Shifted during the Persian Gulf War A classic example of the tradeoff confronting the Fed was the crisis in the Persian Gulf during the summer of 1990. There were numerous indications of a possible recession in the United States, encouraging the Fed to implement a loose-money policy. However, the abrupt increase in oil prices at that time placed upward pressure on U.S. inflation. Consequently, the Fed was less willing to use a loose-money policy because of the additional inflationary pressure that would result.

How the Fed's Emphasis Shifted during 2001–2004 The tradeoffs involved in monetary policy can be understood by considering the Fed's decisions during the 2001–2004 period, as shown in Exhibit 5.7, which summarizes the Fed's main concern at the time of each FOMC meeting. In 2001 when economic conditions were weak, the Fed not only decided to reduce the federal funds target rate at several meetings, but also announced that it was maintaining a bias toward loosening in case the economy remained sluggish. This meant that the Fed was ready to reduce the federal funds rate even further if necessary to stimulate the economy.

From January to December 2001, the FOMC reduced the targeted federal funds rate 10 times, resulting in a cumulative decline of 4.25 percent in the targeted federal funds rate. As the federal funds rate was reduced, other market interest rates declined as well. Each reduction in the targeted federal funds rate reflected an effort by the Fed to encourage more borrowing and spending by consumers and businesses. The large cumulative reduction in interest rates was unusual for a one-year period.

During this period, the economy did not respond to the Fed's interest rate reductions, which is why the Fed continued to reduce rates. One reason for the limited effect on the economy may be that the Fed was focusing on influencing short-term interest rates rather than long-term interest rates. Exhibit 5.8 shows the impact on the targeted federal funds rate over this period along with the Treasury bill (T-bill) rate and a 10-year Treasury bond rate. Notice that in November 2000, short-term interest rates exceeded the 10-year Treasury bond rate, reflecting a downward-sloping yield curve. As the Fed reduced the targeted federal funds rate, the T-bill rate declined along with it, but the Treasury bond rate was less responsive. Consequently, the short-term rates declined below the 10-year Treasury bond rate by 2001, as the bond rate was hardly affected. Other long-term interest rates also remained stable over this period. To the extent that corporations rely on long-term funding to support most of their projects, their cost of borrowing was not significantly reduced over this period. The Fed's effects on the economy might have been stronger had it been able to reduce long-term interest rates during this period.

After the economy failed to respond as hoped in 2001, the Fed reduced the federal funds target rate twice more in 2002 and 2003. Finally, the economy began to show

http://www.federalreserve.gov Click on "federal funds rate." Shows recent changes in the federal funds target rate.

EXHIBIT 5.7 Sample of Conclusions of FOMC Meetings

Meeting	Signs of Economic Growth or Inflation	Action Taken on Federal Funds Target Rate (FFTR)
Early January 2001 (Conference Call Meeting)	Retail sales were weak through the holiday season. The major concern was the weak economy.	Decreased **FFTR** by .5%
Late January 2001	The high-technology sector continued to show weakness. The overall economy showed more signs of weakness. The major concern was the weak economy.	Decreased **FFTR** by .5%
March 2001	Consumer spending increased slightly, but manufacturing orders declined as firms tried to reduce the inventories that had accumulated in recent months. The major concern was the weak economy.	Decreased **FFTR by .5%**
April 2001 (Conference Call Meeting)	Consumer spending leveled off. The major concern was the weak economy.	Decreased **FFTR by .5%**
May 2001	The economy weakened further, but inflation increased slightly. The major concern was the weak economy.	Decreased **FFTR by .5%**
June 2001	There were some signs of improvement, but consumer spending was still low. The major concern was the weak economy.	Decreased **FFTR by .25%**
August 2001	The economy remained sluggish, and there were mixed signals about consumer spending.	Decreased **FFRR by .25%**
September 2001	On September 11, the terrorist attack on the U.S. caused concern that economic conditions would deteriorate. The Fed decided on September 17 (before stock markets reopened) to reduce interest rates.	Decreased **FFTR by .5%**
October 2001	The economy weakened further, as businesses and consumers reduced their travel and spending.	Decreased **FFTR by .5%**
December 2001	Productivity was still low; inflation was also low.	Reduced FFTR by .25%
November 2002	The economy was still not showing strong signs of recovery; the threat of inflation remained low.	Reduced FFTR by .5%
June 2003	The economy had improved but did not show sustainable growth; inflationary expectations were low.	Reduced FFTR by .25%
January 2004	The economy was improving, but since inflation was low, there was no need to raise interest rates.	No change
March 2004	The economy continued to improve while inflation remained low.	No change
May 2004	The economy continued to improve while inflation remained low.	No change
June 2004	The economy continued to improve, but there was concern that inflation could increase in the future.	Increased FFTR by .25%
August 2004	There were signs of higher inflation, partially due to an increase in oil prices. The economy was stable.	Increased FFTR by .25%

some signs of improvement, and by 2004, economic growth was strong, the Fed's focus began to shift from concern about the economy to concern about the potential for higher inflation. In June 2004, the Fed increased the targeted federal funds rate.

Economic Indicators Monitored by the Fed

The Fed monitors various economic indicators. The most important are economic growth indicators and inflation indicators, both of which are discussed next.

EXHIBIT 5.8

Impact of the Fed on Short-
Term versus Long-Term
Rates

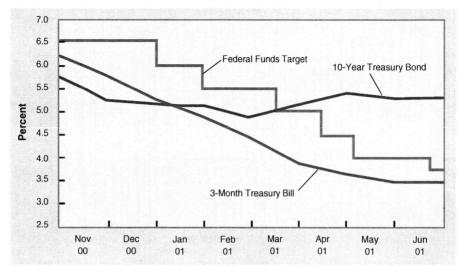

Source: *Monetary Trends,* Federal Reserve Bank of St. Louis, September 2001.

Indicators of Economic Growth

The Fed monitors various indicators of economic growth because high economic growth
creates a more prosperous economy and can result in lower unemployment. GDP, which
measures the total value of goods and services produced during a specific period, is
measured each month. It serves as the most direct indicator of economic growth in the
United States. The level of production adjusts in response to changes in consumers' demand for goods and services. A high production level indicates strong economic growth
and can result in an increased demand for labor (lower unemployment).

The Fed also monitors national income, which is the total income earned by firms
and individual employees during a specific period. A strong demand for U.S. goods and
services results in a large amount of income to firms and employees.

The unemployment rate is monitored as well, because one of the Fed's primary goals
is to maintain a low rate of unemployment in the United States. The unemployment
rate does not necessarily indicate the degree of economic growth, however, because it
measures only the number and not the types of jobs that are being filled. It is possible
to have a substantial reduction in unemployment during a period of weak economic
growth if new low-paying jobs are created during that period.

Several other indexes serve as indicators of growth in specific sectors of the U.S.
economy, including an industrial production index, a retail sales index, and a home
sales index. A composite index combines various indexes to indicate economic growth
across sectors. In addition to the many indicators reflecting recent conditions, the Fed
may also desire to use forward-looking indicators, such as consumer confidence sur-
veys, to forecast future economic growth.

Indicators of Inflation

Producer and Consumer Price Indexes The Fed closely monitors price indexes and
other indicators to assess the U.S. inflation rate. The producer price index represents
prices at the wholesale level, and the consumer price index represents prices paid by consumers (retail level). There is a lag time of about one month after the period being

measured due to the time required to compile price information for the indexes. Nevertheless, financial markets closely monitor the price indexes because they may be used to forecast inflation, which affects nominal interest rates and the prices of some securities. Agricultural price indexes indicate recent price movements in grains, fruits, and vegetables. Housing price indexes indicate recent price movements in homes and rental properties.

Other Indicators In addition to price indexes, there are several other indicators of inflation. Wage rates are periodically reported in various regions of the United States. Because wages and prices are highly correlated over the long run, wages can indicate price movements. Oil prices can signal future inflation because they affect the costs of some forms of production, as well as transportation costs and the prices paid by consumers for gasoline.

The price of gold is closely monitored because gold prices tend to move in tandem with inflation. Some investors buy gold as a hedge against future inflation. Therefore, a rise in gold prices may signal the market's expectation that inflation will increase.

In some cases, indicators of economic growth are also used to indicate inflation. For example, the release of several favorable employment reports may arouse concern that the economy will overheat and cause demand-pull inflation. Although these reports offer favorable information about economic growth, their information about inflation is unfavorable. The financial markets can be adversely affected by such reports, as investors anticipate that the Fed will have to increase interest rates to reduce the inflationary momentum.

How the Fed Uses Indicators

When the Fed meets to decide on its monetary policy, it assesses the most recent reports of all economic growth indicators and inflation indicators. The Fed uses the indicators to anticipate how economic conditions will change and then determines what monetary policy would be appropriate under these conditions. When economic indicators suggest that economic conditions are weak and getting weaker, the Fed is more willing to use an expansionary monetary policy (especially if inflation is low). When economic indicators suggest that productivity and employment are near full capacity, the Fed tends to reduce money supply growth. If the Fed notices that agricultural prices have risen because of adverse weather conditions, it may expect this form of inflation to be temporary and will not adjust its monetary policy. If numerous indicators suggest a large increase in the prices of all goods and services, however, the Fed may implement a monetary policy that is designed to reduce inflation.

Index of Leading Economic Indicators

In addition to the economic indicators monitored by the Fed, the Conference Board publishes indexes of leading, coincident, and lagging economic indicators, which are widely followed by market participants. **Leading economic indicators** are used to predict future economic activity. Usually, three consecutive monthly changes in the same direction in these indicators suggest a turning point in the economy. **Coincident economic indicators** tend to reach their peaks and troughs at the same time as business cycles. **Lagging economic indicators** tend to rise or fall a few months after business-cycle expansions and contractions.

The Conference Board is an independent, not-for-profit membership organization whose stated goal is to create and disseminate knowledge about management and the

EXHIBIT 5.9

The Conference Board's
Indexes of Leading,
Coincident, and Lagging
Indicators

Leading Index

1. Average weekly hours, manufacturing

2. Average weekly initial claims for unemployment insurance

3. Manufacturers' new orders, consumer goods and materials

4. Vendor performance, slower deliveries diffusion index

5. Manufacturers' new orders, nondefense capital goods

6. Building permits, new private housing units

7. Stock prices, 500 common stocks

8. Money supply, M2

9. Interest rate spread, 10-year Treasury bonds less federal funds

10. Index of consumer expectations

Coincident Index

1. Employees on nonagricultural payrolls

2. Personal income less transfer payments

3. Industrial production

4. Manufacturing and trade sales

Lagging Index

1. Average duration of unemployment

2. Inventories to sales ratio, manufacturing and trade

3. Labor cost per unit of output, manufacturing

4. Average prime rate

5. Commercial and industrial loans

6. Consumer installment credit to personal income ratio

7. Consumer price index for services

marketplace to help businesses strengthen their performance and better serve society. The Conference Board conducts research, convenes conferences, makes forecasts, assesses trends, and publishes information and analyses. A summary of the Conference Board's leading, coincident, and lagging indexes is provided in Exhibit 5.9.

Lags in Monetary Policy

One of the main reasons that monetary policy is so complex is the lag between the time an economic problem arises and the time it will take for an adjustment in money supply growth to solve it. Three specific lags are involved. First, there is a **recognition lag,** or the lag between the time a problem arises and the time it is recognized. Most economic problems are initially revealed by statistics, not actual observation. Because economic statistics are reported only periodically, they will not immediately signal a problem. For example, the unemployment rate is reported monthly. A sudden increase in unemployment may not be detected until the end of the month when statistics reveal the problem. And even though most economic variables are updated monthly, the recognition lag could still be longer than one month. For example, if unemployment increases slightly each month for two straight months, the Fed may not necessarily act on this information, because the information may not appear to be significant. Only after a few more months of steadily increasing unemployment might the Fed recognize that a serious problem exists. In such a case, the recognition lag may be four months or longer.

The lag from the time a serious problem is recognized until the time the Fed implements a policy to resolve it is known as the **implementation lag.** Then, even after the Fed implements a policy, there will be an **impact lag** until the policy has its full impact on the economy. For example, an adjustment in money supply growth may have an immediate impact on the economy to some degree, but its full impact may not be manifested until a year or so after the adjustment.

These lags hinder the Fed's control of the economy. Suppose the Fed uses a loose-money policy to stimulate the economy and reduce unemployment. By the time the implemented monetary policy begins to take effect, the unemployment rate may have already reversed itself as a result of some other outside factors (such as a weakened dollar that increased foreign demand for U.S. goods and created U.S. jobs). Thus, the more serious problem may now be inflation (because the economy is heating up again), which may be further ignited by the loose-money policy. Without monetary policy lags, implemented policies would have a higher rate of success.

Assessing the Impact of Monetary Policy

Financial market participants will not all necessarily react to monetary policy in the same manner because they trade different securities. Monetary policy may have a different expected or actual impact on long-term mortgage rates than on corporate and municipal bond rates, money market rates, and stock prices. Exhibit 5.10 shows the various components of the financial environment that are affected by monetary policy. As this exhibit suggests, interest rates are the most influential economic variable on the performance of many financial markets.

Even financial market participants that trade the same securities may react differently to monetary policy because they may have different expectations about the policy's impact on economic variables. They have only limited success in forecasting economic variables because of the difficulty in forecasting (1) money supply movements and (2) how future money supply movements will affect interest rates. Each of these forecasting aspects is discussed in the following subsections.

Forecasting Money Supply Movements

Business periodicals from time to time specify the weekly ranges of M1 and M2 based on the Fed's most recent disclosure of its target range. The Fed is less concerned about meeting its targets on a weekly basis than about meeting its long-term targets. Nevertheless, some financial participants compare the actual money supply levels with weekly ranges that can be estimated from the Fed's longer-term target ranges. Weekly ranges represent the path that the Fed would follow over time if it were to move toward its targets at a constant rate. For example, if the target growth range is specified as 4 to 6 percent annually, the money supply should grow at a weekly rate of between 4%/52 and 6%/52 (given 52 weeks per year). If the Fed consistently over- or undershoots these weekly ranges, it may desire to offset the deviations at some point in the future.

EXHIBIT 5.10

How Monetary Policy
Affects Financial Conditions

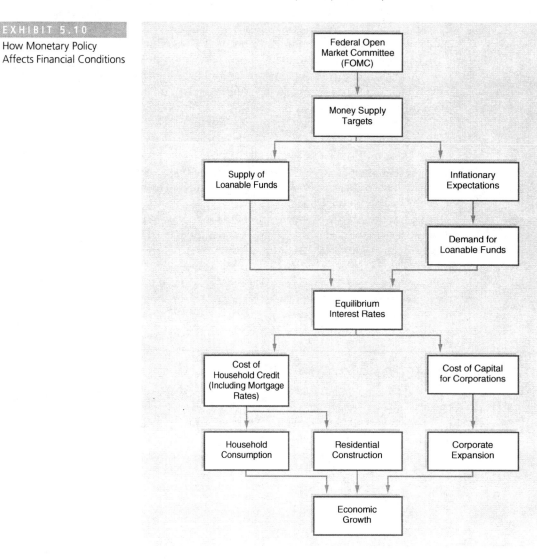

When the actual money supply falls outside the target range, it could be because of a change in the Fed's range that has not yet been publicly announced. The Fed may be meeting its new targets, while financial market participants believe it plans to adjust the money supply to meet its previously announced range. Normally, the Fed attempts to avoid revising target ranges because if it changes them too often, it may lose some credibility. Persistent changes might suggest that it is unsure of how money supply fluctuations affect the economy.

Improved Communication from the Fed Before 1999, the Fed did not disclose what happened at an FOMC meeting until several weeks after the meeting. It was hoping to stabilize financial markets by concealing its change in monetary policy. However, market participants took positions based on their speculation about the Fed's monetary policy. The uncertainty and speculation caused volatile price movements in the securities markets just after an FOMC meeting.

Since 1999, the Fed has been more willing to disclose its conclusions. It now immediately communicates the results of its FOMC meetings. Specifically, it announces the amount by which the federal funds target rate was changed (if at all) and also mentions whether its next action will likely involve a tightening or loosening of the money supply. If the Fed is more concerned about future inflation, it says its position is a "tightening bias," implying that it may raise the federal funds target rate and tighten the money supply if inflation remains high. If it is more concerned about future unemployment (weak economic conditions), it says its position is a "loosening bias," implying that it may lower the federal funds target rate and loosen the money supply if the economy weakens further.

ILLUSTRATION At 7:30 A.M. on September 17, 2001, the FOMC determined that it should adjust monetary policy. The U.S. stock markets, which had been closed since the attack on the United States on September 11, were about to reopen. Anticipating that the attack would further weaken the already faltering U.S. economy, the FOMC decided to reduce the federal funds target rate by 50 basis points (.50 percent). A portion of the Fed's information release on September 17, 2001, is provided here:

> *"The Federal Open Market Committee decided today to lower its target for the federal funds rate by 50 basis points to 3 percent. In a related action, the Board of Governors approved a 50 basis point reduction in the discount rate to 2.5 percent. The Federal Reserve will continue to supply unusually large volumes of liquidity to the financial markets as needed, until a more normal functioning market is restored. . . . Even before the tragic events last week, employment, production, and business spending remained weak, and last week's events have the potential to damp spending further. . . . For the forseeable future, the Fed continues to believe that against the background of its long-run goals of price stability and sustainable economic growth and of the information currently available, the risks are weighted mainly toward conditions that may generate economic weakness."*

The Fed issues such a release after each FOMC meeting, not just under unusual circumstances as in this example. Notice that the Fed not only immediately announced its intentions, but indicated that it anticipated continued economic weakness (see the last sentence). It was implying that it was positioned to loosen money supply growth further if the economy continued to weaken.

http://www.federalreserve
.gov Schedule of FOMC
meetings and minutes
of previous FOMC
meetings.

Because of the quick and clear communication following FOMC meetings, financial market participants do not have to guess at the FOMC's decision. Before the meetings, however, they still speculate about what the FOMC will do. Moreover, after the meeting they still have to assess the impact of the Fed's actions on security valuations. When the Fed releases information about a future tightening or loosening bias, market participants attempt to assess the probability that the Fed will implement that policy in the future.

Forecasting the Impact of Monetary Policy

Even if financial market participants correctly anticipate changes in money supply movements, they may not be able to predict future economic conditions. The historical relationship between the money supply and economic variables has not remained perfectly stable over time. Some adjustments in the money supply caused by the behavior of depositors can distort the relationship between money supply levels and economic growth. For example, when interest rates decline, some individuals may withdraw their deposits to invest in stocks. Consequently, the money supply level (as measured by M2) decreases even though the funds are still invested in the United States. This type of reduction in the money supply may not have the same effect on the economy as when funds are pulled out of the economy by the Fed. Thus, the relationship between the money supply and economic growth is affected.

Impact of Monetary Policy across Financial Markets Because monetary policy can have a strong influence on interest rates and economic growth, it affects the securities traded in all financial markets. The type of influence monetary policy can have on each financial market is summarized in Exhibit 5.11. Some institutions hire economists to focus on assessing monetary policy so that they can determine how their various securities portfolios will be affected.

EXHIBIT 5.11 Impact of Monetary Policy across Financial Markets

Type of Financial Market	Relevant Factors Influenced by Monetary Policy	Key Institutional Participants
Money market	**Interest rates:** • Affect the secondary market values of existing money market securities. • Affect yields on newly issued money market securities. **Economic growth:** • Affects the risk premium on money market securities.	Commercial banks, savings institutions, credit unions, money market funds, insurance companies, finance companies, pension funds.
Bond market	**Interest rates:** • Affect the secondary market values of existing bonds. • Affect the yields offered on newly issued bonds. **Economic growth:** • Affects the risk premium on corporate and municipal bonds.	Commercial banks, savings institutions, bond mutual funds, insurance companies, finance companies, pension funds.
Mortgage market	**Interest rates:** • Affect the demand for housing and therefore the demand for mortgages. • Affect the secondary market values of existing mortgages. • Affect the interest rates on new mortgages. **Economic growth:** • Affects the demand for housing and therefore the demand for mortgages. • Affects the risk premium on mortgages.	Commercial banks, savings institutions, credit unions, insurance companies, pension funds.
Stock market	**Interest rates:** • Affect the required return on stocks and therefore the market values of stocks. **Economic growth:** • Affects projections for corporate earnings and therefore stock values.	Stock mutual funds, insurance companies, pension funds.
Foreign exchange	**Interest rates:** • Affect the demand for currencies and therefore the values of currencies, which in turn affect currency option prices.	Institutions that are exposed to exchange rate risks.

Integrating Monetary and Fiscal Policies

Although the Fed has the power to make decisions without the approval of the presidential administration, the Fed's monetary policy is commonly influenced by the administration's fiscal policies. In some situations, the Fed and the administration have used complementary policies to resolve economic problems. In other situations, they have used conflicting policies. A framework for explaining how monetary policy and fiscal policy affect interest rates is shown in Exhibit 5.12. As this framework shows, monetary policy not only has a direct effect on the supply of funds, but can have an indirect effect on the supply of funds and on the demand for funds. Although fiscal policy typically influences the demand for loanable funds, monetary policy normally has a larger impact on the supply of loanable funds.

History

The presidential administration has historically been most concerned with maintaining strong economic growth and low unemployment. The Fed generally shared the same

EXHIBIT 5.12

Framework for Explaining How Monetary Policy and Fiscal Policy Affect Interest Rates over Time

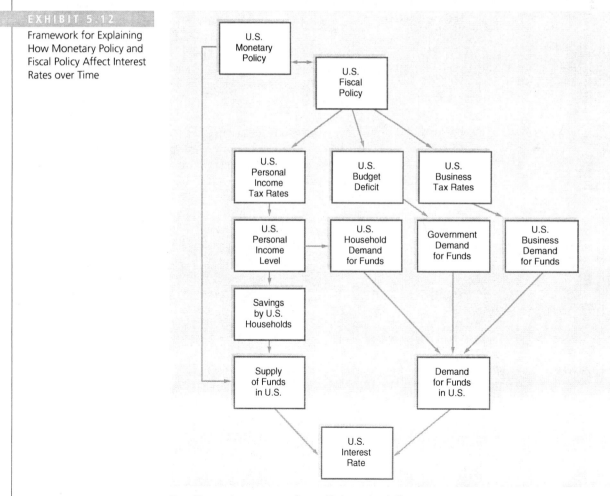

Note: Diagram does not account for possible international effects.

concern in the early 1970s. A year before President Nixon's reelection in 1972, the economy was somewhat stagnant, and inflation was higher than in previous years. The Nixon administration and the Fed combined their power to resolve these problems. The administration enforced wage-price controls (although many exceptions were allowed) to limit inflation, while the Fed used a stimulative monetary policy to reduce unemployment. Although such a stimulative policy can normally lead to higher inflation, the wage-price controls temporarily prevented inflationary consequences. By the 1972 presidential election, economic conditions had improved, which was a primary reason for Nixon's victory. When the wage-price controls were lifted in 1973, however, inflation increased.

By 1980, inflation was close to 10 percent annually, and unemployment was also high. At that time, the administration attempted to stimulate the economy by reducing tax rates. In contrast, the Fed used a relatively tight monetary policy to reduce inflation. As expected, the tight-money policy slowed economic growth and effectively reduced inflation. Although the Fed was given partial credit for lowering inflation, it was also criticized for causing the recession and for not resolving the recession as quickly as it could have. Had the Fed used a stimulative policy to eliminate the recession, however, inflation could have reignited.

The Fed's increased concern for inflation during the early 1980s relative to the 1970s was partially attributed to the appointment of Paul Volcker as chairman in 1979. Volcker was a strong believer in reducing the inflationary spiral that had persisted throughout the 1970s. Financial market participants who understood Volcker's beliefs may have been able to forecast the Fed's anti-inflationary monetary policy during the early 1980s.

The Fed and the administration sometimes differ on whether economic growth (and unemployment) or inflation deserves the most attention. Some of their most intense arguments occurred during the 1982 recession. The administration was being criticized for the high unemployment rate and blamed the Fed's tight monetary policy for keeping interest rates high and reducing the level of borrowing and spending. The Fed argued that the high interest rates were due to the large budget deficit resulting from the administration's fiscal policy. It also argued that the administration was putting too much emphasis on satisfying short-term goals for political (election) reasons and not enough emphasis on reducing inflation.

The Fed ultimately loosened the money supply in 1983, which reduced interest rates, increased economic growth, and pulled the United States out of the recession. In recent years, there has been less disagreement between the Fed and the administration, as the inflation rate and unemployment rate have been maintained at relatively low levels.

Monetizing the Debt

An ongoing dilemma faced by the Fed is whether to help finance the federal budget deficit that has been created by fiscal policy.

ILLUSTRATION   Consider a situation in which the administration decides to implement a new fiscal policy that will result in a larger federal deficit than was originally expected. The Fed must first assess the potential impact that this new fiscal policy will have on the economy. A likely concern of the Fed is the possibility of a crowding-out effect, in which excessive borrowing by the Treasury crowds out other potential borrowers (such as households or corporations) in competing for whatever loanable funds are available. This can cause higher interest rates and therefore may restrict economic growth. The Fed may counter by loosening the money supply, which might offset the increased demand for loanable funds by the federal government. This action is known as **monetizing the**

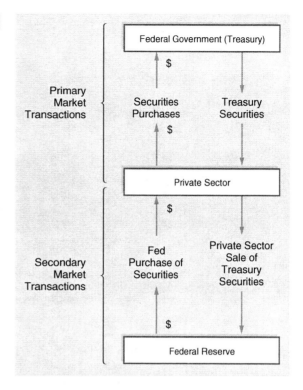

EXHIBIT 5.13

Fed's Process of Monetizing the Debt

debt, as the Fed is partially financing the federal deficit. Exhibit 5.13 illustrates how this works. As the Treasury issues new securities in the primary market to finance the deficit, there may be upward pressure on interest rates. The Fed could offset this pressure by using open market operations to purchase Treasury securities (from government securities dealers) in the secondary market. Before the Fed monetizes the debt, it may first monitor how the additional borrowing by the Treasury is affecting interest rates. If there is no significant change in interest rates, the Fed may decide not to intervene.

When the Fed purchases Treasury securities, the Treasury must repurchase the securities at maturity just as if an individual or a firm owned them. Thus, Treasury securities held by the Fed still reflect debt from the Treasury's perspective. The Treasury may sometimes prefer that the Fed monetize the debt, however, because if it does not, interest rates could rise and reduce economic growth.

The Fed may prefer not to monetize the debt because this strategy requires higher money supply growth, which could ignite inflation. If the Fed does not monetize the debt, however, a weak economy may be more likely.

Market Assessment of Integrated Policies

Financial market participants must consider the potential policies of both the administration (fiscal) and the Fed (monetary) when assessing future economic conditions. Exhibit 5.14 provides a broad overview of how the participants monitor monetary and fiscal policy actions. The participants forecast the type of monetary and fiscal policies that will be implemented and then determine how these anticipated policies will affect future economic conditions. For example, they must forecast shifts in the supply of and

EXHIBIT 5.14
Simultaneous Assessment
of Fiscal and Monetary
Policies

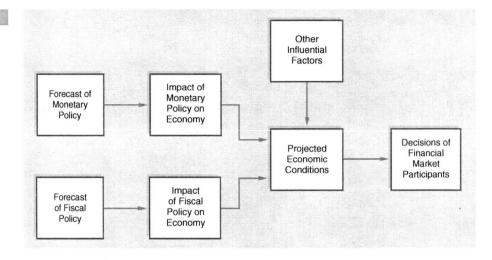

demand for loanable funds, which requires a forecast of the factors that affect such funds. The supply of loanable funds can be affected by the Fed's adjustment of the money supply or any changes in tax policies by the administration. The demand for loanable funds is affected by any change in inflationary expectations, which can be influenced by fluctuations in the money supply or aggregate spending. In addition, the demand for loanable funds is affected by government expenditures. Tax rate changes could also affect the demand for loanable funds if they affect the incentive for firms or individuals to borrow.

Once forecasts of the supply of and demand for loanable funds are completed, interest rate movements can be forecast. Interest rate projections are necessary to forecast the aggregate demand for goods and services, which will influence the level of economic growth, the unemployment rate, and the inflation rate. Other factors not directly related to government policies, such as oil prices and labor contract situations, also have an impact on the economic variables, and these, too, have to be considered.

Global Effects of Monetary Policy

GL🌐BALASPECTS   Financial market participants must recognize that the type of monetary policy implemented by the Fed is somewhat dependent on various international factors, as explained next.

Impact of the Dollar

A weak dollar can stimulate U.S. exports, discourage U.S. imports, and therefore stimulate the U.S. economy. In addition, it tends to exert inflationary pressure in the United States. Thus, the Fed is less likely to use a stimulative monetary policy when the dollar is weak. A strong dollar tends to reduce inflationary pressure but also dampens the U.S. economy. Therefore, the Fed is more likely to use a stimulative policy during a strong-dollar period.

Impact of Global Economic Conditions

The Fed recognizes that economic conditions are integrated across countries, so it considers prevailing global economic conditions when conducting monetary policy. When global economic conditions are strong, foreign countries purchase more U.S. imports and can stimulate the U.S. economy. When global economic conditions are weak, the foreign demand for U.S. imports weakens.

In 2001, when the United States experienced a very weak economy, the economies of many other countries were also weak. The Fed's decision to lower U.S. interest rates and stimulate the U.S. economy was partially driven by these weak global economic conditions. The Fed recognized that the United States would not receive any stimulus from other countries (such as a strong demand for U.S. imports) where income and aggregate spending levels were also relatively low.

Transmission of Interest Rates

International flows of funds can also affect the Fed's monetary policy. If there is upward pressure on U.S. interest rates that can be offset by foreign inflows of funds, the Fed may not feel compelled to use a loose-money policy. However, if foreign investors reduce their investment in U.S. securities, the Fed may be forced to intervene to prevent interest rates from rising.

Given the international integration in money and capital markets, a government's budget deficit can affect interest rates of various countries. This concept, referred to as **global crowding out,** is illustrated in Exhibit 5.15. An increase in the U.S. budget deficit causes an outward shift in the federal government demand for U.S. funds and therefore in the aggregate demand for U.S. funds (from D_1 to D_2). This crowding-out effect forces the U.S. interest rate to increase from i_1 to i_2 if the supply curve (S) is unchanged. As U.S. rates rise, they attract funds from investors in other countries, such as Germany and Japan. As foreign investors use more of their funds to invest in U.S. securities, the supply of available funds in their respective countries declines. Consequently, there is upward . pressure on non-U.S. interest rates as well. The impact will be most pronounced on those countries whose investors are most likely to be attracted to the higher U.S. interest rates. The possibility of global crowding out has caused national governments to criticize one another for large budget deficits.

Fed Policy during the Asian Crisis

Although the Fed's objectives normally focus on the United States, it recognizes that the economic growth of foreign countries can influence U.S. economic growth, and vice versa. This complicates the determination of the proper monetary policy to impose. For

EXHIBIT 5.15 Illustration of Global Crowding Out

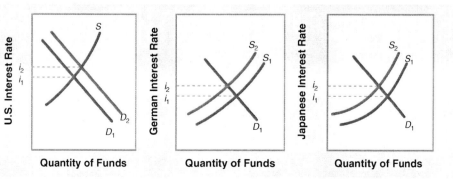

example, during the Asian crisis in the late 1990s, the Fed may have lowered U.S. interest rates more than it would have without the crisis. Although there was some concern that the lower rates would lead to higher U.S. inflation, a greater concern was that if rates were not lowered, the United States would experience a weak economy, which would be transmitted to other countries. The lower U.S. interest rates provided some stimulus to the U.S. economy, offsetting the reduction in U.S. economic growth due to lower demand for U.S. exports during the crisis, and also helped to sustain the U.S. demand for foreign exports. Thus, the Fed's monetary policy was not only influenced by international conditions, but also had an influence on those conditions.

SUMMARY

■ The Keynesian theory suggests how the Fed can affect the interaction between the demand for money and the supply of money, which affects interest rates, aggregate spending, and economic growth. As the Fed increases the money supply, interest rates should decline, which results in more aggregate spending (because of cheaper financing rates) and higher economic growth. As the Fed decreases the money supply, interest rates should increase, which results in less aggregate spending (because of higher financing rates), lower economic growth, and lower inflation.

■ The Monetarist approach suggests that excess growth in the money supply can cause inflationary expectations. Therefore, expansionary monetary policy by the Fed may have limited effects because increasing the money supply may also result in an increased demand for money (in response to higher inflationary expectations). Thus, interest rates may not necessarily be controlled by the Fed's adjustment in the money supply, and the impact of monetary policy on aggregate spending is questionable.

■ A stimulative monetary policy is likely to increase economic growth, but may also cause higher inflation. A restrictive monetary policy is likely to reduce inflation, but may also reduce economic growth. Thus, the Fed faces a tradeoff when implementing monetary policy. Given a possible tradeoff, the Fed tends to assess whether the potential benefits of any proposed monetary policy outweigh the potential adverse effects.

■ Financial market participants attempt to forecast the Fed's future monetary policies and the effects of these policies on economic conditions. Using this information, they can determine how their security holdings would be affected and can adjust their security portfolios accordingly.

■ The proper monetary policy may be dependent on the prevailing fiscal policy. If the fiscal policy involves excessive government borrowing, there is upward pressure on interest rates, and a loose monetary policy may be necessary to offset that pressure on interest rates. However, such a strategy could cause higher inflation in the long run.

POINT COUNTER-POINT

Can the Fed Prevent U.S. Recessions?

Point Yes. The Fed has the power to reduce market interest rates and can therefore encourage more borrowing and spending. In this way, it stimulates the economy.

Counter-Point No. When the economy is weak, individuals and firms are unwilling to borrow regardless of the interest rate. Thus, the borrowing (by those who are qualified) and spending will not be influenced by the Fed's actions. The Fed should not intervene, but should let the economy work itself out of a recession.

Who Is Correct? Use InfoTrac or some other source search engine to learn more about this issue. Offer your own opinion on this issue.

QUESTIONS AND APPLICATIONS

1. **Impact of Monetary Policy** How does the Fed's monetary policy affect economic conditions?

2. **Tradeoffs of Monetary Policy** Describe the economic tradeoff faced by the Fed in achieving its economic goals.

3. **Choice of Monetary Policy** When does the Fed use a loose-money policy, and when does it use a tight-money policy? What is a criticism of a loose-money policy? What is the risk of using a monetary policy that is too tight?

4. **Keynesian Approach** Briefly summarize the pure Keynesian philosophy and identify the key variable considered.

5. **Monetarist Approach** Briefly summarize the Monetarist approach.

6. **Fed Control** Why may the Fed have difficulty in controlling the economy in the manner desired? Be specific.

7. **Lagged Effects of Monetary Policy** Compare the recognition lag and the implementation lag.

8. **Fed's Control of Inflation** Assume that the Fed's primary goal is to cure inflation. How can it use open market operations to achieve its goal? What is a possible adverse effect of this action by the Fed (even if it achieves its goal)?

9. **Monitoring Money Supply** Why do financial market participants closely monitor money supply movements? Why do financial market participants who monitor monetary policy have only limited success in forecasting economic variables?

10. **Fed's Monetary Policy** Why would the Fed try to avoid frequent changes in the money supply?

11. **Impact of Money Supply Growth** Explain why an increase in the money supply can affect interest rates in different ways. Include the potential impact of the money supply on the supply of and demand for loanable funds when answering this question.

12. **Confounding Effects** What factors might be considered by financial market participants who are assessing whether an increase in money supply growth will affect inflation?

13. **Monetizing the Debt** Explain what monetizing the debt means. How can this action improve economic conditions? What is the risk involved?

ADVANCED QUESTIONS

14. **Interpreting the Fed's Monetary Policy** When the Fed increases money supply to lower the federal funds rate, will the cost of capital of U.S. companies be reduced? Explain how the segmented markets theory regarding the term structure of interest rates could influence the degree of which the Fed's monetary policy affects long-term interest rates.

15. **Monetary Policy Today** Assess the economic situation today. Is the administration more concerned with reducing unemployment or inflation? Does the Fed have a similar opinion? If not, is the administration publicly criticizing the Fed? Is the Fed publicly criticizing the administration? Explain.

16. **Impact of Foreign Policies** Why might a foreign government's policies be closely monitored by investors in other countries, even if the investors plan no investments in that country? Explain how monetary policy in one country can affect interest rates in other countries.

17. **Monetary Policy during the War in Iraq** Consider the likely discussion that was occurring in the FOMC meetings during the war in Iraq in 2003. The U.S. economy was weak at that time. Do you think the FOMC should have proposed a loose-money policy or a tight-money policy once the war began? This war could have resulted in major damage to oil wells. Explain why this possible effect would have received much attention at the FOMC meetings. If this possibility was perceived to be highly likely at the time of the meetings, explain how it may have complicated the decision about monetary policy at that time. Given the conditions stated in this question, would you have suggested that the Fed use a tight-money policy, a loose-money policy, or a stable-money policy? Support your decision with logic, and acknowledge any adverse effects of your decision.

18. **Economic Indicators** Stock market conditions serve as a leading economic indicator. Assuming the U.S. economy is currently in a recession, discuss the implications of this indicator. Why might this indicator possibly be inaccurate?

Interpret the following statements made by Wall Street analysts and portfolio managers:

a. "Lately, the Fed's policies are driven by gold prices and other indicators of the future rather than by recent economic data."

b. "The Fed cannot boost money growth at this time because of the weak dollar."

c. "The Fed's fine-tuning may distort the economic picture."

Review the website http://www.federalreserve.gov/fomc with a focus on the activities of the FOMC.

When is the FOMC scheduled to meet next? How many more times will the FOMC meet this year? Succinctly summarize the minutes of the last meeting. What did the FOMC discuss at the last meeting? Did the FOMC make any changes in the current monetary policy? What is the FOMC's current monetary policy?

Forecasting Monetary Policy As a manager of a firm, you are concerned about a potential increase in interest rates, which would reduce the demand for your firm's products. The Fed is scheduled to meet in one week to assess economic conditions and set monetary policy. Economic growth has been high, but inflation has also increased from 3 percent to 5 percent (annualized) over the last four months. The level of unemployment is very low and cannot possibly go much lower.

a. Given the situation, is the Fed likely to adjust monetary policy? If so, how?

b. Recently, the Fed has allowed the money supply to expand beyond its long-term target range. Does this affect your expectation of what the Fed will decide at its upcoming meeting?

c. Assume that the Fed has just learned that the Treasury will need to borrow a larger amount of funds than originally expected. Explain how this information may affect the degree to which the Fed changes the monetary policy.

FLOW OF FUNDS EXERCISE

Anticipating Fed Actions

Recall that Carson Company has obtained substantial loans from finance companies and commercial banks. The interest rate on the loans is tied to market interest rates and is adjusted every six months. Because of its expectations of a strong U.S. economy, Carson plans to grow in the future by expanding its business and through acquisitions. It expects that it will need substantial long-term financing and plans to borrow additional funds either through loans or by issuing bonds. It is also considering the issuance of stock to raise funds in the next year.

An economic report just noted the strong growth in the economy, which has caused the economy to be close to full employment. In addition, the report estimated that the annualized inflation rate increased to 5 percent, up from 2 percent last month. The factors

that caused the higher inflation (shortages of products and shortages of labor) are expected to continue.

a. How will the Fed's monetary policy change based on the report?

b. How will the likely change in the Fed's monetary policy affect Carson's future performance? Could it affect Carson's plans for future expansion?

c. Explain how a tight monetary policy could affect the amount of funds borrowed at financial institutions by deficit units such as Carson Company. How might it affect the credit risk of deficit units such as Carson Company? How might it affect the performance of financial institutions that provide credit to deficit units such as Carson Company?

WSJ EXERCISE

Market Assessment of Fed Policy

Review the "Credit Markets" section in a recent issue of *The Wall Street Journal* (listed in the index on the first page). Summarize the market assessments of the Fed.

Also summarize the market's expectations about future interest rates. Are these expectations based primarily on the Fed's monetary policy or on other factors?

Part II Integrative Problem

Fed Watching

This problem requires an understanding of the Fed (Chapter 4) and monetary policy (Chapter 5). It also requires an understanding of how economic conditions affect interest rates and securities prices (Chapters 2 and 3).

Like many other investors, you are a "Fed watcher," who constantly monitors any actions taken by the Fed to revise monetary policy. You believe that three key factors affect interest rates. Assume that the most important factor is the Fed's monetary policy. The second most important factor is the state of the economy, which influences the demand for loanable funds. The third factor is the level of inflation, which also influences the demand for loanable funds. Because monetary policy can affect interest rates, it affects economic growth as well. By controlling monetary policy, the Fed influences the prices of all types of securities.

The following information is available:

- Economic growth has been consistently strong over the past few years but is beginning to slow down.
- Unemployment is as low as it has been in the past decade but has risen slightly over the past two quarters.
- Inflation has been about 5 percent per year for the past few years.
- The dollar has been strong.
- Oil prices have been very low.

Yesterday, an event occurred that you believe will cause much higher oil prices in the United States and a weaker U.S. economy in the near future. You plan to determine whether the Fed will respond to the economic problems that are likely to develop.

You have reviewed previous economic slowdowns caused by a decline in the aggregate demand for goods and services and found that each slowdown precipitated a loose-money policy by the Fed. Inflation was 3 percent or less in each of the previous economic slowdowns. Interest rates generally declined in response to these policies, and the U.S. economy improved.

Assume that the Fed's philosophy regarding monetary policy is to maintain economic growth and low inflation. There does not appear to be any major fiscal policy forthcoming that will have a major effect on the economy. Thus, the future economy is up to the Fed. The Fed's present policy is to maintain a 2 percent annual growth rate in the money supply. You believe that the economy is headed toward a recession unless the Fed uses a very stimulative monetary policy, such as a 10 percent annual growth rate in the money supply.

The general consensus of economists is that the Fed will revise its monetary policy to stimulate the economy for three reasons: (1) it recognizes the potential costs of higher unemployment if a recession occurs, (2) it has consistently used a stimulative policy in the past to prevent recessions, and (3) the administration has been pressuring the Fed to use a stimulative monetary policy. Although you consider the opinions of the economists, you plan to make your own assessment of the Fed's future policy. Two quarters ago, GDP declined by 1 percent. Last quarter, GDP declined again by 1 percent. Thus, there is clear evidence that the economy has recently slowed down.

Questions

1   Do you think that the Fed will use a stimulative monetary policy at this point? Explain.

2   You maintain a large portfolio of U.S. bonds. You believe that if the Fed does not revise its monetary policy, the U.S. economy will continue to decline. If the Fed stimulates the economy at this point, you believe that you would be better off with stocks than with bonds. Based on this information, do you think you should switch to stocks? Explain.

4

Money Markets

oney markets are used to facilitate the transfer of short-term funds from individuals, corporations, or governments with excess funds to those with deficient funds. Even investors who focus on long-term securities tend to hold some money market securities. Money markets enable financial market participants to maintain liquidity.

The specific objectives of this chapter are to:

■ provide a background on the most popular money market securities,

■ explain how money markets are used by institutional investors,

■ explain the valuation and risk of money market securities, and

■ explain how money markets have become globally integrated.

Money Market Securities

Securities with maturities within one year are referred to as **money market securities.** They are issued by corporations and governments to obtain short-term funds. They are originally issued in the primary market through a telecommunications network that informs investors that new securities are for sale.

Money market securities are commonly purchased by corporations (including financial institutions) and government agencies that have funds available for a short-term period. Because money market securities have a short-term maturity and can typically be sold in the secondary market, they provide liquidity to investors. Most firms and financial institutions maintain some holdings of money market securities for this reason.

The more popular money market securities are:

■ Treasury bills
■ Commercial paper
■ Negotiable certificates of deposit
■ Repurchase agreements
■ Federal funds
■ Banker's acceptances

Each of these instruments is described in turn.

Treasury Bills

When the U.S. government needs to borrow funds, the U.S. Treasury frequently issues short-term securities known as Treasury bills (or T-bills). These are sold weekly through an auction. One-year T-bills are issued on a monthly basis. The par value (amount received by investors at maturity) of T-bills was historically a minimum of $10,000, but is now $1,000 and in multiples of $1,000 thereafter. T-bills are sold at a discount from par value, and the gain to an investor holding a T-bill until maturity is the difference between par value and the price paid.

T-bills are attractive to investors because they are backed by the federal government and therefore are virtually free of credit (default) risk. Another attractive feature of T-bills is their liquidity, which is due to their short maturity and strong secondary market. Existing T-bills can be sold in the secondary market through government securities dealers, who profit by purchasing the bills at a slightly lower price than the price at which they sell them.

Investors in Treasury Bills Depository institutions commonly invest in T-bills so that they can retain a portion of their funds in assets that can easily be liquidated if they suddenly need to accommodate deposit withdrawals. Other financial institutions also invest in T-bills in the event that they need cash because cash outflows exceed cash inflows. Individuals with substantial savings invest in T-bills for liquidity purposes. Many individuals invest in T-bills indirectly by investing in money market funds, which in turn purchase large amounts of T-bills. Corporations invest in T-bills so that they have easy access to funding if they incur sudden unanticipated expenses.

Pricing Treasury Bills The price that an investor will pay for a T-bill with a particular maturity is dependent on the investor's required rate of return on that T-bill. That price is determined as the present value of the future cash flows to be received. Since the T-bill does not generate interest payments, the value of a T-bill is the present value of the par value.

ILLUSTRATION If investors require a 7 percent annualized return on a one-year T-bill, the price that they will be willing to pay is

$$P = \$10,000/1.07$$
$$= \$9,345.79$$

Since T-bills do not pay interest, the investors should pay this price so that the $10,000 they receive a year later will have to generate a 7 percent return.

To price a T-bill with a maturity shorter than one year, the annualized return can be reduced by the fraction of the year in which funds will be invested.

ILLUSTRATION If investors require a 6 percent annualized return on a six-month T-bill, this reflects a 3 percent unannualized return over six months. The price that they would be willing to pay is

$$P = \$10,000/1.03$$
$$= \$9,708.74$$

EXHIBIT 6.1

Example of a Treasury Bill Application

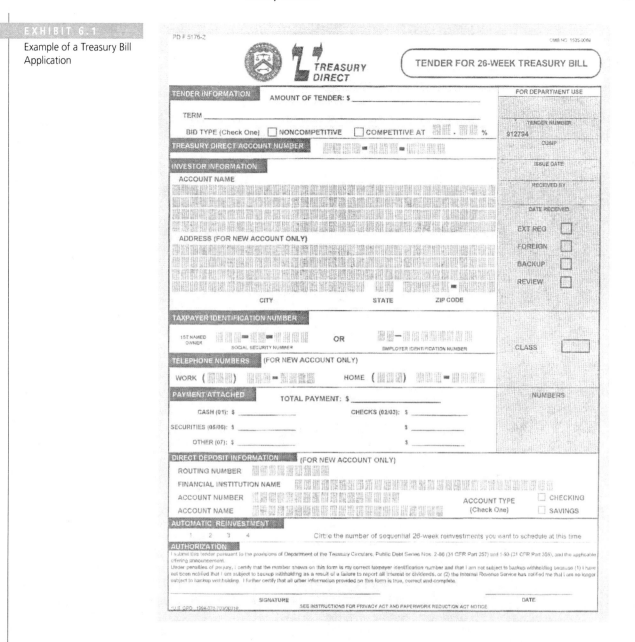

Treasury Bill Auction The primary T-bill market is an auction by mail. Investors submit bids on T-bill applications for the maturity of their choice. Exhibit 6.1 shows an example of a 26-week T-bill application. Applications can be obtained at no charge from a Federal Reserve district or branch bank. Alternatively, investors can ask a broker or a commercial bank to obtain and send in the application for them. The fee charged for this service normally ranges from $25 to $75.

Financial institutions can arrange to submit their bid for T-bills (and other Treasury securities) online using the Treasury Automated Auction Processing System (TAAPS-Link). Financial institutions using this arrangement set up an account with the Treasury. Then they can select the specific maturity and face value that they desire and submit their bids electronically. Payments to the Treasury are withdrawn electronically from the account, and payments received from the Treasury when the securities mature are deposited electronically into the account.

At the weekly auctions, the Treasury offers 13-week (three-month) and 26-week (six-month) T-bills. As of July 2001, the Treasury began to include 4-week T-bills in some of the weekly auctions. The 4-week T-bills are offered when the Treasury anticipates a short-term cash deficiency over a given month. The Treasury also periodically offers some other T-bills with shorter-term maturities, called cash management bills.

At the auctions, investors have the option of bidding competitively or noncompetitively. The Treasury has a specified amount of funds that it plans to borrow during the 13- or 26-week period, and this dictates the amount of T-bill bids that it will accept for that maturity. Investors who wish to ensure that their bids will be accepted can use noncompetitive bids. Noncompetitive bidders are limited to purchasing T-bills with a maximum par value of $1 million per auction, however. Consequently, large corporations typically make competitive bids so they can purchase larger amounts.

After accounting for noncompetitive bids, the Treasury accepts the highest competitive bids first and works it way down until it has generated the amount of funds from competitive bids that it needs. Any bids below that cutoff point are not accepted. Since 1998, the Treasury applies the lowest accepted bid price to all competitive bids that are accepted and to all noncompetitive bids. Thus, the price paid by competitive and noncompetitive bidders reflects the lowest price of the competitive bids. Competitive bids are still submitted because, as noted above, many bidders want to purchase more T-bills than the maximum that can be purchased on a noncompetitive basis.

The results of the weekly auction of 13-week and 26-week T-bills are summarized in major daily newspapers each Tuesday and are also provided online at the Treasury's Public Debt website. Some of the more commonly reported statistics are the dollar amount of applications and Treasury securities sold, the average price of the accepted competitive bids, and the coupon equivalent (annualized yield) for investors who paid the average price.

The results of a recent T-bill auction are shown in Exhibit 6.2. At each auction, the prices paid for six-month T-bills are significantly lower than the prices paid for three-month T-bills because the investment term is longer. The lower price results in a higher unannualized yield that compensates investors for their longer-term investment.

Estimating the Yield As explained earlier, T-bills do not offer coupon payments but are sold at a discount from par value. Their yield is influenced by the difference between the selling price and the purchase price. If an investor purchases a newly issued T-bill and holds it until maturity, the return is based on the difference between the par value and the purchase price. If the T-bill is sold prior to maturity, the return is based on the difference between the price for which the bill was sold in the secondary market and the purchase price.

http://www.ny.frb.org
Click on "Treasury Direct."
Results of recent Treasury
bill auctions.

http://www.federalreserve
.gov/releases
Links to a database of
Treasury bill rates over time

EXHIBIT 6.2

Example of Treasury Bill
Auction Results

	13-Week Treasury Bill Auction	26-Week Treasury Bill Auction
Applications	$22,685,977,000	$23,991,246,000
Accepted bids	$9,022,977,000	$8,005,496,000
Average price of accepted bids (per $100 par value)	$98.792	$97.508
Coupon equivalent (yield)	4.918%	5.139%

Source: *The Wall Street Journal.* See *The Wall Street Journal* on any Tuesday for the information pertaining to Monday's Treasury bill auction.

The annualized yield from investing in a T-bill (Y_T) can be determined as

$$Y_T = \frac{SP - PP}{PP} \times \frac{365}{n}$$

where $\quad SP$ = selling price

$\qquad PP$ = purchase price

$\qquad n$ = number of days of the investment (holding period)

ILLUSTRATION An investor purchases a T-bill with a six-month (182-day) maturity and $10,000 par value for $9,600. If this T-bill is held to maturity, its yield is

$$Y_T = \frac{\$10,000 - \$9,600}{\$9,600} \times \frac{365}{182} = 8.36\%$$

If the T-bill is sold prior to maturity, the selling price and therefore the yield are dependent on market conditions at the time of the sale.

Suppose the investor plans to sell the T-bill after 120 days and forecasts a selling price of $9,820 at that time. The expected annualized yield based on this forecast is

$$Y_T = \frac{\$9,820 - \$9,600}{\$9,600} \times \frac{365}{120} = 6.97\%$$

The higher the forecasted selling price, the higher the expected annualized yield.

Estimating the Treasury Bill Discount Business periodicals frequently quote the T-bill discount (or T-bill rate) along with the T-bill yield. The T-bill discount represents the percent discount of the purchase price from par value (Par) for newly issued T-bills and is computed as

$$\text{T-bill discount} = \frac{\text{Par} - PP}{\text{Par}} \times \frac{360}{n}$$

A 360-day year is used to compute the T-bill discount.

ILLUSTRATION Using the information from the previous example, the T-bill discount is

$$\text{T-bill discount} = \frac{\$10,000 - \$9,600}{\$10,000} \times \frac{360}{182} = 7.91\%$$

For a newly issued T-bill that is held to maturity, the T-bill yield will always be higher than the discount. The difference occurs because the purchase price is the denominator of the yield equation, while the par value is the denominator of the T-bill discount equation, and the par value will always exceed the purchase price of a newly issued T-bill. In addition, the yield formula uses a 365-day year versus a 360-day year for the discount computation.

Commercial Paper

Commercial paper is a short-term debt instrument issued only by well-known, creditworthy firms and is typically unsecured. It is normally issued to provide liquidity or finance a firm's investment in inventory and accounts receivable. The issuance of commercial paper is an alternative to short-term bank loans. Financial institutions such as finance companies and bank holding companies are major issuers of commercial paper.

The minimum denomination of commercial paper is usually $100,000. The typical denominations are in multiples of $1 million. Maturities are normally between 20 and 45 days but can be as short as one day or as long as 270 days. The 270-day maximum is due to a Securities and Exchange Commission (SEC) ruling that paper with a maturity exceeding 270 days must be registered.

Because of the high minimum denomination, individual investors rarely purchase commercial paper directly although they may invest in it indirectly by investing in money market funds that have pooled the funds of many individuals. Money market funds are major investors in commercial paper. An active secondary market for commercial paper does not exist. However, it is sometimes possible to sell the paper back to the dealer who initially helped to place it. In most cases, investors hold commercial paper until maturity.

Ratings Since commercial paper is issued by corporations that are susceptible to business failure, the commercial paper could possibly default. The risk of default is influenced by the issuer's financial condition and cash flow. Investors can attempt to assess the probability that commercial paper will default by monitoring the issuer's financial condition. The focus is on the issuer's ability to repay its debt over the short term because the payments will be completed within a short-term period. The rating serves as an indicator of the potential risk of default. Money market funds can invest only in commercial paper that has a top-tier or second-tier rating, and second-tier paper cannot represent more than 5 percent of their assets. Thus, corporations can more easily place commercial paper that is assigned a top-tier rating. The ratings are assigned by rating agencies such as Moody's Investor Service, Standard & Poor's Corporation, and Fitch Investor Service.

A higher-risk classification can increase a corporation's commercial paper rate by as much as 150 basis points (1.5 percent). The difference has reached 150 basis points during some recessions but has been less than 50 basis points over other periods.

From 1970 to 1988, there were only a few major defaults on commercial paper. In 1989, however, several major issuers defaulted, including Wang Labs, Lomas Financial, and Drexel Burnham Lambert. All of these issues were rated highly until the default. These defaults led to a growing number of commercial paper issues (called **junk commercial paper**) that were rated low or not rated at all. In the last decade, the number of defaults on commercial paper has been very low.

Volume of Commercial Paper The volume of commercial paper issued over time is shown in Exhibit 6.3. In general, the volume of commercial paper issued has increased substantially over time. The tendency of firms to use commercial paper for short-term financing is influenced by their ability to obtain funds in the commercial paper market at a relatively low cost. The volume of commercial paper commonly declines during recessions when corporations tend to borrow less. In addition, some corporations are viewed as having higher default risk on their debt during recessions, so any new commercial paper they issued would be assigned a low rating. This would raise the cost of financing with commercial paper or perhaps even prevent the corporations from obtaining funds in the commercial paper market. Notice in Exhibit 6.3 how the volume of commercial paper declined substantially in 2001 and 2002, when economic conditions were very weak.

Placement Some firms place commercial paper directly with investors. Ford Motor Credit and other firms have recently sold their commercial paper online to investors.

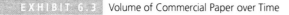 Volume of Commercial Paper over Time

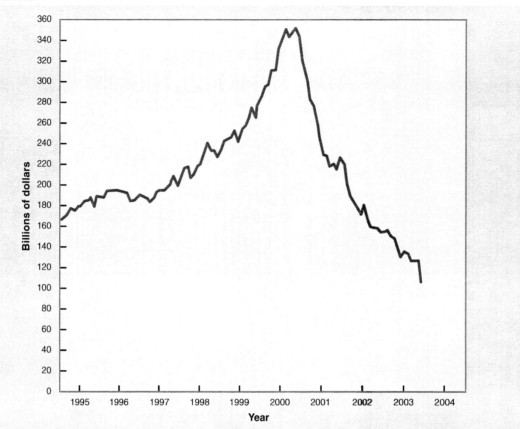

Source: Federal Reserve.

Other firms rely on commercial paper dealers to sell their commercial paper, at a cost of usually one-eighth of 1 percent of the face value. This transaction cost is generally less than it would cost to establish a department within the firm to place commercial paper directly. Companies that frequently issue commercial paper may reduce expenses by creating such a department, however. Most nonfinancial companies prefer to use commercial paper dealers rather than in-house resources to place their commercial paper. Their liquidity needs, and therefore their commercial paper issues, are cyclical, so they would use an in-house direct-placement department only a few times during the year. Finance companies typically maintain an in-house department because they frequently borrow in this manner.

Backing Commercial Paper Issuers of commercial paper typically maintain backup lines of credit in case they cannot roll over (reissue) commercial paper at a reasonable rate because, for example, their assigned rating was lowered. A backup line of credit provided by a commercial bank allows the company the right (but not the obligation) to borrow a specified maximum amount of funds over a specified period of time. The fee for the line can either be a direct percentage of the total accessible credit (such as 0.5 percent) or be in the form of required compensating balances (such as 10 percent of the line).

Estimating the Yield At a given point in time, the yield on commercial paper is slightly higher than the yield on a T-bill with the same maturity because commercial paper carries some credit risk and is less liquid. Like T-bills, commercial paper is sold at a discount from par value. The nominal return to investors who retain the paper until maturity is the difference between the price paid for the paper and the par value. Thus, the yield received by a commercial paper investor can be determined in a manner similar to the T-bill yield, although a 360-day year is usually used.

If an investor purchases 30-day commercial paper with a par value of $1,000,000 for a price of $990,000, the yield ($Y_{cp}$) is

$$Y_{cp} = \frac{\$1,000,000 - \$990,000}{\$990,000} \times \frac{360}{30}$$

$$= 12.12\%$$

When a firm plans to issue commercial paper, the price (and therefore yield) to investors is uncertain. Thus, the cost of borrowing funds is uncertain until the paper is issued. Consider the case of a firm that plans to issue 90-day commercial paper with a par value of $5,000,000. It expects to sell the commercial paper for $4,850,000. The yield it expects to pay investors (its cost of borrowing) is estimated to be

$$Y_{cp} = \frac{Par - PP}{PP} \times \frac{360}{n}$$

$$= \frac{\$5,000,000 - \$4,850,000}{\$4,850,000} \times \frac{360}{90}$$

$$= 12.37\%$$

When firms sell their commercial paper at a lower (higher) price than projected, their cost of raising funds will be higher (lower) than they initially anticipated. For example, if the firm initially sold the commercial paper for $4,865,000, the cost of borrowing would have been about 11.1 percent. (Check the math as an exercise.)

Ignoring transaction costs, the cost of borrowing with commercial paper is equal to the yield earned by investors holding the paper until maturity. The cost of borrowing can be adjusted for transaction costs (charged by the commercial paper dealers) by subtracting the nominal transaction fees from the price received.

Some corporations prefer to issue commercial paper rather than borrow from a bank because it is usually a cheaper source of funds. Yet, even the large creditworthy corporations that are able to issue commercial paper normally obtain some short-term loans from commercial banks in order to maintain a business relationship with them.

Commercial Paper Yield Curve The commercial paper yield curve represents the yield offered on commercial paper at various maturities. The curve is typically established for a maturity range from 0 to 90 days because most commercial paper has a maturity within that range. This yield curve is important because it may influence the maturity that is used by firms that issue commercial paper and by the institutional investors that purchase commercial paper. The shape of this yield curve could be roughly drawn from the short-term range of the traditional Treasury yield curve. However, that curve is graphed over a long time period, so it is difficult to derive the precise shape of a yield curve over a three-month range from that graph.

The same factors that affect the Treasury yield curve from 0 to 10 years affect the commercial paper yield curve, but are applied to very short-term horizons. In particular, expectations of interest over the next few months can influence the commercial paper yield curve.

Assume that many firms that issue paper and institutional investors expect that the one-month interest rate as of one month from now will be much higher than the prevailing one-month interest rate. Firms that want to issue commercial paper would likely prefer to issue two-month or three-month commercial paper so that they can lock in the yield that they will pay and avoid having to refinance in one month. Conversely, institutional investors would likely prefer to invest in one-month commercial paper so that they can reinvest their funds at the higher yields (if interest rates rise as expected) when the commercial paper matures. Thus, there will be a surplus of funds in the one-month commercial market, but stronger demand and a smaller supply of funds in the two-month market. The result is an upward-sloping commercial paper yield curve, as shown in the top panel of Exhibit 6.4. A downward-sloping commercial paper yield curve could exist if firms and investors expected that short-term interest rates would decrease. In this case, firms would prefer to issue commercial paper with shorter term maturities, which would result in a higher annualized yield for these maturities.

EXHIBIT 6.4

Commercial Paper Yield Curve

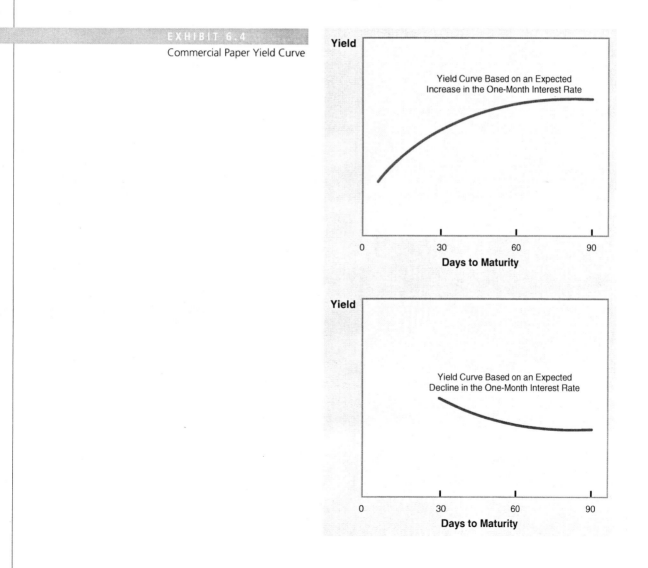

The shapes of the yield curves of other money market securities will be similar to the shape of the yield curve for commercial paper because the financial institutions that participate in the commercial paper market tend to participate in all of these markets.

Negotiable Certificates of Deposit (NCDs)

Negotiable certificates of deposit (NCDs) are certificates that are issued by large commercial banks and other depository institutions as a short-term source of funds. The minimum denomination is $100,000, although a $1 million denomination is more common. Nonfinancial corporations often purchase NCDs. Although NCD denominations are typically too large for individual investors, they are sometimes purchased by money market funds that have pooled individual investors' funds. Thus, money market funds allow individuals to be indirect investors in NCDs, creating a more active NCD market.

Maturities on NCDs normally range from two weeks to one year. A secondary market for NCDs exists, providing investors with some liquidity. However, institutions prefer not to have their newly issued NCDs compete with their previously issued NCDs that are being resold in the secondary market. An oversupply of NCDs for sale can force them to sell their newly issued NCDs at a lower price.

Placement Some issuers place their NCDs directly; others use a correspondent institution that specializes in placing NCDs. Another alternative is to sell NCDs to securities dealers, who in turn resell them. A portion of unusually large issues is commonly sold to NCD dealers. Normally, however, NCDs can be sold to investors directly at a higher price.

Premium NCDs must offer a premium above the T-bill yield to compensate for less liquidity and safety. The premiums are generally higher during recessionary periods. The premiums also reflect the market's perception about the safety of the financial system.

Yield NCDs provide a return in the form of interest along with the difference between the price at which the NCD is redeemed (or sold in the secondary market) and the purchase price. Given that an institution issues an NCD at par value, the annualized yield that it will pay is the annualized interest rate on the NCD. If investors purchase this NCD and hold it until maturity, their annualized yield is the interest rate. However, the annualized yield can differ from the annualized interest rate for investors who either purchase or sell the NCD in the secondary market instead of holding it from inception until maturity.

ILLUSTRATION An investor purchased an NCD a year ago in the secondary market for $970,000. He redeems it today upon maturity and receives $1,000,000. He also receives interest of $40,000. His annualized yield (Y_{NCD}) on this investment is

$$Y_{NCD} = \frac{SP - PP + \text{interest}}{PP}$$

$$= \frac{\$1,000,000 - \$970,000 + \$40,000}{\$970,000}$$

$$= 7.22\%$$

Repurchase Agreements

With a repurchase agreement (or repo), one party sells securities to another with an agreement to repurchase the securities at a specified date and price. In essence, the repo transaction represents a loan backed by the securities. If the borrower defaults on the loan, the lender has claim to the securities. Most repo transactions use government securities, although some involve other securities such as commercial paper or NCDs. A **reverse repo** refers to the purchase of securities by one party from another with an agreement to sell them. Thus, a repo and a reverse repo can refer to the same transaction but from different perspectives. These two terms are sometimes used interchangeably, so a transaction described as a repo may actually be a reverse repo.

Financial institutions such as banks, savings and loan associations, and money market funds often participate in repurchase agreements. Many nonfinancial institutions are active participants as well. Transaction amounts are usually for $10 million or more. The most common maturities are from one day to 15 days and for one, three, and six months. A secondary market for repos does not exist. Some firms in need of funds will set the maturity on a repo to be the minimum time period for which they need temporary financing. If they still need funds when the repo is about to mature, they will borrow additional funds through new repos and use these funds to fulfill their obligation on maturing repos.

Placement Repo transactions are negotiated through a telecommunications network. Dealers and repo brokers act as financial intermediaries to create repos for firms with deficient and excess funds, receiving a commission for their services.

When the borrowing firm can find a counterparty to the repo transaction, it avoids the transaction fee involved in having a government securities dealer find the counterparty. Some companies that commonly engage in repo transactions have an in-house department for finding counterparties and executing the transactions. These same companies that borrow through repos may, from time to time, serve as the lender. That is, they purchase the government securities and agree to sell them back in the near future. Because the cash flow of any large company changes on a daily basis, it is not unusual for a firm to act as an investor one day (when it has excess funds) and a borrower the next (when it has a cash shortage).

Estimating the Yield The repo rate is determined by the difference between the initial selling price of the securities and the agreed-upon repurchase price, annualized with a 360-day year.

An investor initially purchased securities at a price (PP) of $9,852,217, with an agreement to sell them back at a price (SP) of $10,000,000 at the end of a 60-day period. The yield (or repo rate) on this repurchase agreement is

$$\text{Repo rate} = \frac{SP - PP}{PP} \times \frac{360}{n}$$

$$= \frac{\$10,000,000 - \$9,852,217}{\$9,852,217} \times \frac{360}{60}$$

$$= 9\%$$

Federal Funds

The federal funds market allows depository institutions to effectively lend or borrow short-term funds from each other at the so-called **federal funds rate.** The federal funds

http://www.federalreserve
.gov/fomc Provides an
excellent summary of the
Fed's adjustment in the
federal funds rate over
time.

rate is the rate charged on federal funds transactions. It is influenced by the supply and demand for funds in the federal funds market. The Federal Reserve adjusts the amount of funds in depository institutions in order to influence the federal funds rate (as explained in Chapter 4) and several other short-term interest rates. All types of firms closely monitor the federal funds rate because the Federal Reserve manipulates it to affect general economic conditions. Many market participants view changes in the federal funds rate as an indicator of potential changes in other money market rates.

The federal funds rate is normally slightly higher than the T-bill rate at any point in time. The negotiations between two depository institutions may take place directly over a communications network or may occur through a federal funds broker. Once a loan transaction is agreed upon, the lending institution can instruct its Federal Reserve district bank to debit its reserve account and to credit the borrowing institution's reserve account by the amount of the loan. If the loan is for just one day, it will likely be based on an oral agreement between the parties, especially if the institutions commonly do business with each other.

Commercial banks are the most active participants in the federal funds market. Federal funds brokers serve as financial intermediaries in the market, matching up institutions that wish to sell (lend) funds with those that wish to purchase (borrow) them. The brokers receive a commission for their service. The transactions are negotiated through a telecommunications network that links federal funds brokers with the participating institutions. Most loan transactions are for $5 million or more and usually have a one- to seven-day maturity (although the loans may often be extended by the lender if the borrower desires more time).

The volume of interbank loans on commercial bank balance sheets over time is an indication of the importance of lending between depository institutions. The interbank loan volume outstanding now exceeds $200 billion.

Banker's Acceptances

A **banker's acceptance** indicates that a bank accepts responsibility for a future payment. Banker's acceptances are commonly used for international trade transactions. An exporter that is sending goods to an importer whose credit rating is not known will often prefer that a bank act as a guarantor. The bank therefore facilitates the transaction by stamping ACCEPTED on a draft, which obligates payment at a specified point in time. In turn, the importer will pay the bank what is owed to the exporter along with a fee to the bank for guaranteeing the payment.

Exporters can hold a banker's acceptance until the date at which payment is to be made, but they frequently sell the acceptance before then at a discount to obtain cash immediately. The investor who purchases the acceptance then receives the payment guaranteed by the bank in the future. The investor's return on a banker's acceptance, like that on commercial paper, is derived from the difference between the discounted price paid for the acceptance and the amount to be received in the future. Maturities on banker's acceptances often range from 30 to 270 days. Because there is a possibility that a bank will default on payment, investors are exposed to a slight degree of credit risk. Thus, they deserve a return above the T-bill yield as compensation.

Because acceptances are often discounted and sold by the exporting firm prior to maturity, an active secondary market exists. Dealers match up companies that wish to sell acceptances with other companies that wish to purchase them. The bid price of dealers is less than their ask price, which creates their spread, or their reward for doing business. The spread is normally between one-eighth and seven-eighths of 1 percent.

EXHIBIT 6.5

Sequence of Steps in the
Creation of a Banker's
Acceptance

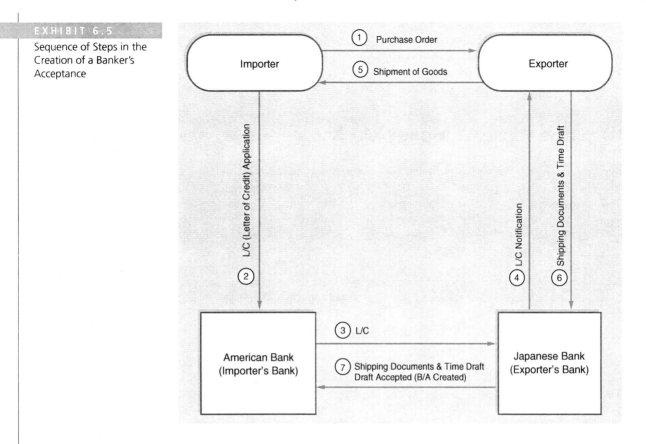

Steps Involved in Banker's Acceptances The sequence of steps involved in a banker's acceptance is illustrated in Exhibit 6.5. To understand these steps, consider the example of a U.S. importer of Japanese goods. First, the importer places a purchase order for the goods (Step 1). If the Japanese exporter is unfamiliar with the U.S. importer, it may demand payment before delivery of goods, which the U.S. importer may be unwilling to make. A compromise may be reached through the creation of a banker's acceptance. The importer asks its bank to issue a **letter of credit (L/C)** on its behalf (Step 2). The L/C represents a commitment by that bank to back the payment owed to the Japanese exporter. Then the L/C is presented to the exporter's bank (Step 3), which informs the exporter that the L/C has been received (Step 4). The exporter then sends the goods to the importer (Step 5) and sends the shipping documents to its bank (Step 6), which passes them along to the importer's bank (Step 7). At this point, the banker's acceptance is created, which obligates the importer's bank to make payment to the holder of the banker's acceptance at a specified future date. The banker's acceptance may be sold to a money market investor at a discount. Potential purchasers of acceptances are short-term investors. When the acceptance matures, the importer pays its bank, which in turn pays the money market investor who presents the acceptance.

The creation of a banker's acceptance allows the importer to receive goods from an exporter without sending immediate payment. The selling of the acceptance creates financing for the exporter. Even though banker's acceptances are often created to facilitate international transactions, they are not limited to money market investors with international experience. Investors who purchase acceptances are more concerned with the credit of the bank that guarantees payment than with the credit of the exporter or importer. For this reason, the credit risk on a banker's acceptance is somewhat similar to that of NCDs issued by commercial banks. Yet, because acceptances have the backing of the bank as well as the importing firm, they may be perceived as having slightly less credit risk than NCDs.

Institutional Use of Money Markets

The institutional use of money market securities is summarized in Exhibit 6.6. Financial institutions purchase money market securities in order to simultaneously earn a return and maintain adequate liquidity. They issue money market securities when experiencing a temporary shortage of cash. Because money markets serve businesses, the average transaction size is very large and is typically executed through a telecommunications network.

Money market securities can be used to enhance liquidity in two ways. First, newly issued securities generate cash. The institutions that issue new securities have created a short-term liability in order to boost their cash balance. Second, institutions that previously purchased money market securities will generate cash upon liquidation of the securities. In this case, one type of asset (the security) is replaced by another (cash).

Most financial institutions maintain sufficient liquidity by holding either securities that have very active secondary markets or securities with short-term maturities. T-bills are the most popular money market instrument because of their marketability, safety, and short-term maturity. Although T-bills are purchased through an auction, other money market instruments are commonly purchased through dealers or specialized brokers. For example, commercial paper is purchased through commercial paper dealers or directly from the issuer, NCDs are usually purchased through brokers specializing in NCDs, federal funds are purchased (borrowed) through federal funds brokers, and repurchase agreements are purchased through repo dealers.

Financial institutions whose future cash inflows and outflows are more uncertain will generally maintain additional money market instruments for liquidity. For this reason,

EXHIBIT 6.6 Institutional Use of Money Markets

Type of Financial Institution	Participation in the Money Markets
Commercial banks and savings institutions	• Bank holding companies issue commercial paper. • Some banks and savings institutions issue NCDs, borrow or lend funds in the federal funds market, engage in repurchase agreements, and purchase T-bills. • Commercial banks create banker's acceptances. • Commercial banks provide backup lines of credit to corporations that issue commercial paper.
Finance companies	• Issue large amounts of commercial paper.
Money market mutual funds	• Use proceeds from shares sold to invest in T-bills, commercial paper, NCDs, repurchase agreements, and banker's acceptances.
Insurance companies	• May maintain a portion of their investment portfolio as money market securities for liquidity.
Pension funds	• May maintain a portion of their investment portfolio as money market securities that may be liquidated when portfolio managers desire to increase their investment in bonds or stocks.

depository institutions such as commercial banks allocate a greater portion of their asset portfolio to money market instruments than pension funds usually do.

Financial institutions that purchase money market securities are acting as a creditor to the initial issuer of the securities. For example, when they hold T-bills, they are creditors to the Treasury. The T-bill transactions in the secondary market commonly reflect a flow of funds between two nongovernment institutions. T-bills represent a source of funds for those financial institutions that liquidate some of their T-bill holdings. In fact, this is the main reason that financial institutions hold T-bills. Liquidity is also the reason financial institutions purchase other money market instruments, including federal funds (purchased by depository institutions), repurchase agreements (purchased by depository institutions and money market funds), banker's acceptances, and NCDs (purchased by money market funds).

Some financial institutions issue their own money market instruments to obtain cash. For example, depository institutions issue NCDs, and bank holding companies and finance companies issue commercial paper. Depository institutions also obtain funds through the use of repurchase agreements or in the federal funds market.

Many money market transactions involve two financial institutions. For example, a federal funds transaction involves two depository institutions. Money market funds commonly purchase NCDs from banks and savings institutions. Repurchase agreements are frequently negotiated between two commercial banks.

Valuation of Money Market Securities

Many types of money market securities make no interest payments but do provide principal at maturity. The value of these money market securities is measured as the present value of the principal payment to be paid at maturity. The discount rate used to discount the money market security is the required rate of return by investors. Thus, the value reflects the present value of a future lump-sum payment.

ILLUSTRATION Assume that a money market security has a par value of $10,000 and a maturity of one year, and that investors require a return of 7 percent on this security. The present value (*PV*) of this security is

$$PV = \$10,000/(1.07)^1$$
$$= \$9,345.79$$

If investors require a 9 percent return on that security instead of 7 percent, its present value will be

$$PV = \$10,000/(1.09)^1$$
$$= \$9,174.31$$

This value is lower than in the previous example because if investors require a higher return, they will be willing to purchase the security only if its price is lower.

If short-term interest rates decline, the required rate of return on money market securities will decline, and the values of money market securities will increase. Although money market security values are sensitive to interest rate movements in the same direction as bonds, they are not as sensitive as bond values to interest rate movements. The lower degree of sensitivity is primarily attributed to the shorter term to maturity. With money market securities, the principal payment will occur in the next year, whereas the principal payment on bonds may be 10 or 20 years away. In other words, an increase in interest rates is not as harmful to a money market security because it will mature soon anyway, and the investor can reinvest the proceeds at the prevailing rate at that time. An increase in interest rates is more harmful to a bond with 20 years until maturity because the investor will be earning a low rate on the bond for the next 20 years.

Explaining Money Market Price Movements

The market price of money market securities (P_m) should equal the present value of their future cash flows. Since money market securities normally do not make periodic interest payments, their cash flows are in the form of one lump-sum payment of principal. Therefore, the market price of a money market security can be determined as

$$P_m = \text{Par}/(1 + k)^n$$

where
Par = par value or principal amount to be provided at maturity

k = required rate of return by investors

n = time to maturity

Since money market securities have maturities of one year or less, n is measured as a fraction of one year.

A change in P_m can be modeled as

$$\Delta P_m = f(\Delta k) \text{ and } \Delta k = f(\Delta R_f, \Delta RP)$$

where
R_f = risk-free interest rate

RP = risk premium

Therefore,

$$\Delta P_m = f(\Delta R_f, \Delta RP)$$

Exhibit 6.7 identifies the underlying forces that can affect the short-term risk-free interest rate (the T-bill rate) and the risk premium and can therefore cause the price of a money market security to change over time. When pricing T-bills, the focus is on the factors that affect the risk-free interest rate, as the risk premium is not needed. Thus, the difference in the required return of a risky money market security (such as commercial paper) versus the T-bill (for a given maturity) is the risk premium, which is influenced by economic, industry, and firm-specific conditions.

Impact of September 11 To understand how the valuations and therefore the yields offered on money market securities can change, consider the effect of the terrorist attack on the United States on September 11, 2001. The economy was weak at the time, and investors anticipated that the event would cause additional weakness. They sold stocks and transferred funds into money market securities such as T-bills and commercial paper. This created an unusually strong demand for money market securities, which placed upward pressure on their price and downward pressure on their yields. At the

EXHIBIT 6.7 Framework for Pricing Money Market Securities

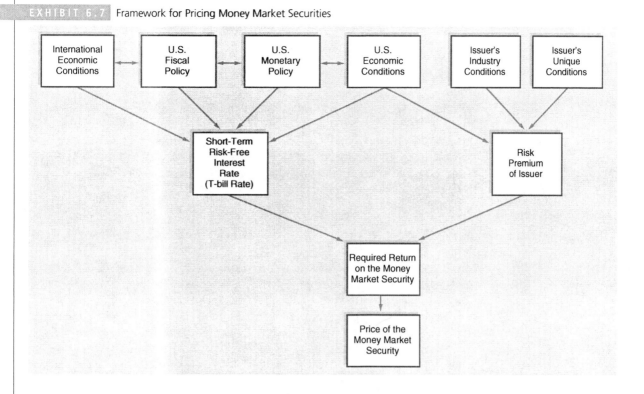

same time investors were taking these actions, the Federal Reserve was acting to add liquidity to the banking system and to reduce the federal funds rate. Consequently, all money market security yields declined to their lowest level in more than 30 years.

Efficiency of Money Market Securities

The money markets are referred to as efficient if the prices of the securities reflect all available information. In general, the money markets are widely perceived to be efficient, in that the prices reflect all available public information. Most money market securities are subject to large trading volume and therefore are monitored by many investors. The price of a money market security such as commercial paper can decline quickly if the issuer suddenly announces financial problems. However, this type of adjustment in price does not reflect a violation of market efficiency. In fact, it is because of market efficiency that the price adjusts so quickly to new information. Most investors buy money market securities because they need liquidity, not because they think they can capitalize on mispricing of the securities. They are more likely to think that they could earn larger gains in other financial markets, but rely on the money markets for liquidity.

Indicators of Future Money Market Security Prices

Money market participants closely monitor economic indicators that may signal future changes in the strength of the economy, which can signal changes in short-term interest rates and in the required return from investing in money market securities. Some of the more closely monitored indicators of economic growth include employment, gross domestic product, retail sales, industrial production, and consumer confidence. An unexpected favorable movement in these indicators tends to create expectations of increased economic growth and higher interest rates, which place downward pressure on prices of money market securities.

Money market participants also closely monitor indicators of inflation, such as the consumer price index and the producer price index. In general, an unexpected increase in these indexes tends to create expectations of higher interest rates and places downward pressure on money market prices. Whenever indicators signal a potential increase in interest rates, money market participants tend to shift their investments into securities with relatively short terms to maturity so that they can receive a higher yield by reinvesting in newly issued securities once interest rates rise.

Risk of Money Market Securities

When corporate treasurers, institutional investors, and individual investors invest in money market securities, they are subject to the risk that the return on their investment will be less than anticipated. The forces that influence price movements of money market securities cannot be perfectly anticipated, so future money market prices (and therefore yields) cannot be perfectly anticipated either. If the money market securities will not be held until maturity, the prices at which they can be sold in the future (and therefore the return on the investment) will depend primarily on the risk-free interest rate and the perceived credit risk at the time the securities are sold. Because the investment horizon for money market securities is short term, the investment is not subject to a major loss in value as a result of an increase in interest rates, but it still faces a potential loss of value if the issuer of the money market security defaults.

At one extreme, if corporate treasurers, institutional investors, and individual investors want to avoid risk, they can purchase T-bills and hold them to maturity, but investors who choose T-bills forgo a higher expected return because T-bills do not need to offer a risk premium. Consequently, investors must weigh the higher potential return of investing in other money market securities against the exposure to risk (that the actual return could be lower than the expected return). Since the risk of a large loss is primarily attributed to the possibility of default, investors commonly invest in money market securities (such as commercial paper) that offer a slightly higher yield than T-bills and are very unlikely to default. Although investors can assess economic and firm-specific conditions to determine the credit risk of an issuer of a money market security, information about the issuer's financial condition is limited.

Measuring Risk

Participants in the money markets can use sensitivity analysis to determine how the value of money market securities may change in response to a change in interest rates.

ILLUSTRATION Assume that Long Island Bank has money market securities with a par value of $100 million that will mature in nine months. Since the bank will need a substantial amount of funds in three months, it wants to know how much cash it will receive from selling these securities three months from now. Assume that it expects the unannualized required rate of return on those securities for the remaining six months to be

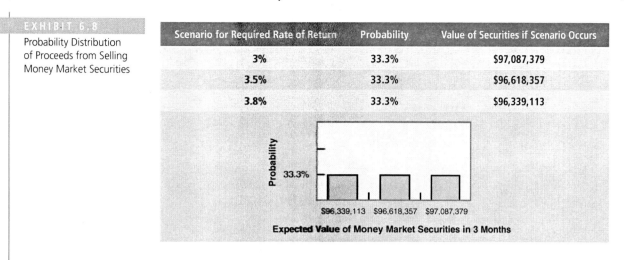

Probability Distribution
of Proceeds from Selling
Money Market Securities

Scenario for Required Rate of Return	Probability	Value of Securities if Scenario Occurs
3%	33.3%	$97,087,379
3.5%	33.3%	$96,618,357
3.8%	33.3%	$96,339,113

3 percent, or 3.5 percent, or 3.8 percent with a 33.3 percent chance for each of these three scenarios.

Exhibit 6.8 shows the probability distribution of the proceeds that Long Island Bank will receive from selling the money market securities in three months, based on the possible scenarios for the required rate of return at that time. Based on this exhibit, the bank expects that it will receive at least $96,339,113, but it could receive more if interest rates (and therefore the required rate of return) are relatively low in three months. By deriving a probability distribution of outcomes, the bank can anticipate whether the proceeds to be received will be sufficient to cover the amount of funds that it needs in three months.

Interaction among Money Market Yields

Companies investing in money markets closely monitor the yields on the various instruments. Because the instruments serve as reasonable substitutes for each other, the investing companies may exchange instruments to achieve a more attractive yield. This causes yields among these instruments to be somewhat similar. If a disparity in yields arises, companies will avoid the low-yield instruments in favor of the high-yield instruments. This places upward pressure on the yields of the low-yield securities and downward pressure on the high-yield securities, causing realignment.

During periods of heightened uncertainty about the economy, investors tend to shift from risky money market securities to Treasury securities. This so-called flight to quality creates a greater differential between yields, as risky money market securities must provide a larger premium to attract investors.

Exhibit 6.9 shows the yields of money market securities over time. The high degree of correlation among security yields is obvious. T-bills consistently offer slightly lower yields than the other securities because they are very liquid and free from credit risk.

Globalization of Money Markets

 GLOBALASPECTS   Market interest rates vary among countries, as shown in Exhibit 6.10. The interest rate differentials occur because geographic markets are somewhat segmented. The interest rates of 12 European countries, however, have converged and are now the same as a result of

EXHIBIT 6.9   Money Market Yields (Averages, Annualized)

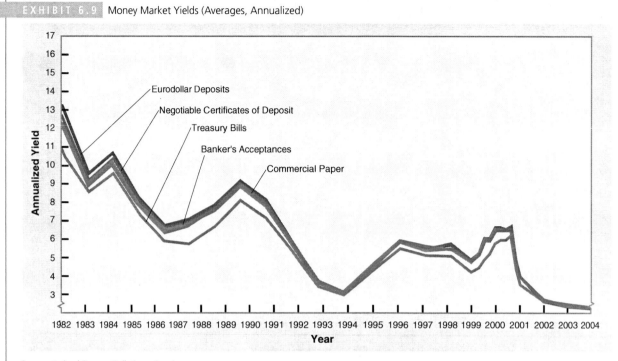

Source: *Federal Reserve Bulletin,* various issues.

the conversion of their currencies to the euro in January 1999. In addition, the interest rates of some other countries have become more highly correlated over time, as the flow of funds between countries has increased. The increase in the flow of funds is attributed to tax differences among countries, speculation on exchange rate movements, and a reduction in government barriers that were previously imposed on foreign investment in securities. U.S. T-bills and commercial paper are very accessible to foreign investors. In addition, securities such as Eurodollar deposits, Euronotes, and Euro-commercial paper are

EXHIBIT 6.10   International Money Market Rates over Time

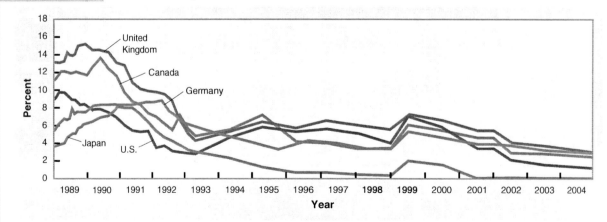

Source: Federal Reserve.

Money Market Rates

A **table** in *The Wall Street Journal* called "Money Rates" provides the interest rates on a wide variety of money market securities. The name of the rate or security is listed in **boldface** type. For securities with several common maturities, the rate on each maturity is disclosed.

Money Rates
Monday, September 27, 2004

The key U. S. and foreign annual interest rates below are a guide to general levels but don't always represent actual transactions.

Commercial Paper

Yields paid by corporations for short-term financing, typically for daily operation

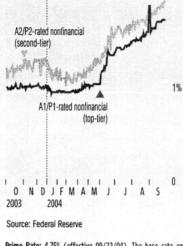

A2/P2-rated nonfinancial (second-tier)

1%

A1/P1-rated nonfinancial (top-tier)

0

O N D J F M A M J J A S
2003   2004

Source: Federal Reserve

Prime Rate: 4.75% (effective 09/22/04). The base rate on corporate loans posted by at least 75% of the nation's 30 largest banks.
Discount Rate (Primary): 2.75% (effective 09/21/04).
Federal Funds: 1.813% high, 1.625% low, 1.375% near closing bid, 1.875% offered. Effective rate: 1.76%. Source: Prebon Yamane (USA) Inc. Federal-funds target rate: 1.750% (effective 09/21/04).
Call Money: 3.50% (effective 09/22/04).
Commercial Paper: Placed directly by General Electric Capital Corp.: 1.76% 30 to 59 days; 1.80% 60 to 89 days; 1.86% 90 to 119 days; 1.93% 120 to 149 days; 1.98% 150 to 174 days; 2.04% 175 to 209 days; 2.08% 210 to 239 days; 2.12% 240 to 263 days; 2.15% 264 to 270 days.
Euro Commercial Paper: Placed directly by General Electric

Capital Corp.: 2.04% 30 days; 2.06% two months; 2.09% three months; 2.12% four months; 2.14% five months; 2.17% six months.
Dealer Commercial Paper: High-grade unsecured notes sold through dealers by major corporations: 1.77% 30 days; 1.84% 60 days; 1.89% 90 days.
Certificates of Deposit: 1.80% one month; 1.92% three months; 2.10% six months.
Bankers Acceptances: 1.78% 30 days; 1.84% 60 days; 1.91% 90 days; 1.99% 120 days; 2.05% 150 days; 2.11% 180 days. Source: Prebon Yamane (USA) Inc.
Eurodollars: 1.80% - 1.78% one month; 1.87% - 1.84% two months; 1.93% - 1.91% three months; 2.02% - 1.98% four months; 2.07% - 2.05% five months; 2.14% - 2.10% six months. Source: Prebon Yamane (USA) Inc.
London Interbank Offered Rates (Libor): 1.8400% one month; 1.9700% three months; 2.1700% six months; 2.4500% one year. Effective rate for contracts entered into two days from date appearing at top of this column.
Euro Libor: 2.08013% one month; 2.11575% three months; 2.20425% six months; 2.37738% one year. Effective rate for contracts entered into two days from date appearing at top of this column.
Euro Interbank Offered Rates (Euribor): 2.081% one month; 2.116% three months; 2.204% six months; 2.379% one year. Source: Reuters.
Foreign Prime Rates: Canada 4.00%; European Central Bank 2.00%; Japan 1.375%; Switzerland 2.47%; Britain 4.75%.
Treasury Bills: Results of the Monday, September 27, 2004, auction of short-term U.S. government bills, sold at a discount from face value in units of $1,000 to $1 million: 1.710% 13 weeks; 1.950% 26 weeks. Tuesday, September 21, 2004 auction: 1.605% 4 weeks.
Overnight Repurchase Rate: 1.69%. Source: Garban Intercapital.
Freddie Mac: Posted yields on 30-year mortgage commitments. Delivery within 30 days 5.38%, 60 days 5.44%, standard conventional fixed-rate mortgages: 2.875%, 2% rate capped one-year adjustable rate mortgages.
Fannie Mae: Posted yields on 30 year mortgage commitments (priced at par) for delivery within 30 days 5.44%, 60 days 5.50%, standard conventional fixed-rate mortgages; 3.30%, 6/2 rate capped one-year adjustable rate mortgages. Constant Maturity Debt Index: 1.941% three months; 2.120% six months; 2.387% one year.
Merrill Lynch Ready Assets Trust: 1.00%.
Consumer Price Index: August, 189.5, up 2.7% from a year ago. Bureau of Labor Statistics.

widely traded throughout the international money markets, as discussed in the following subsections.

Eurodollar Deposits and Euronotes

As corporations outside the United States (especially in Europe) increasingly engaged in international trade transactions in U.S. dollars, the U.S. dollar deposits in non-U.S. banks (called **Eurodollar certificates of deposit** or Eurodollar CDs) grew. Furthermore, because interest rate ceilings were historically imposed on dollar deposits in U.S. banks, corporations with large dollar balances often deposited their funds overseas to receive a higher yield.

Eurodollar CD volume has grown substantially over time, as the U.S. dollar is used as a medium of exchange in a significant portion of international trade and investment transactions. Some firms overseas receive U.S. dollars as payment for exports and invest in Eurodollar CDs. Because these firms may need dollars to pay for future imports, they retain dollar-denominated deposits rather than convert dollars to their home currency.

In the so-called **Eurodollar market,** banks channel the deposited funds to other firms that need to borrow them in the form of Eurodollar loans. The deposit and loan transactions in Eurodollars are typically $1 million or more per transaction, so only governments and large corporations participate in this market. Because transaction amounts are large, investors in the market avoid some costs associated with the continuous small transactions that occur in retail-oriented markets. In addition, Eurodollar CDs are not subject to reserve requirements, which means that banks can lend out 100 percent of the deposits that arrive. For these reasons, the spread between the rate banks pay on large Eurodollar deposits and what they charge on Eurodollar loans is relatively small. Consequently, interest rates in the Eurodollar market are attractive for both depositors and borrowers. The rates offered on Eurodollar deposits are slightly higher than the rates offered on NCDs.

A secondary market for Eurodollar CDs exists, allowing the initial investors to liquidate their investment if necessary. The growth in Eurodollar volume has made the secondary market more active.

Investors in fixed-rate Eurodollar CDs are adversely affected by rising market interest rates, while issuers of these CDs are adversely affected by declining rates. To deal with this interest rate risk, **Eurodollar floating-rate CDs** (called **FRCDs**) have been used in recent years. The rate adjusts periodically to the London Interbank Offer Rate (LIBOR), which is the interest rate charged on interbank dollar loans. As with other floating-rate instruments, the rate on FRCDs ensures that the borrower's cost and the investor's return reflect prevailing market interest rates.

Over time, the volume of deposits and loans denominated in other foreign currencies has also grown because of increased international trade, increased flows of funds among subsidiaries of multinational corporations, and existing differences among country regulations on bank deposit rates. Consequently, the so-called **Eurocurrency market** was developed; it is made up of several banks (called **Eurobanks**) that accept large deposits and provide large loans in foreign currencies. These same banks also make up the **Eurocredit market,** which is distinguished from the Eurocurrency market mainly by the longer maturities on loans.

The Eurobanks participating in the Eurocurrency market are located not only in Europe but also in the Bahamas, Canada, Japan, Hong Kong, and some other countries. Since 1978, Eurocurrency deposits at commercial banks have more than quadrupled. Over this time period, the value of dollar deposits has represented between 70 percent and 80 percent of the market value of all Eurocurrency deposits. In recent years, the percentage has declined slightly because of the growth in nondollar Eurocurrency deposits.

Short-term **Euronotes** are issued in bearer form, with common maturities of one, three, and six months. Typical investors in Euronotes often include the Eurobanks that are hired to place the paper. These Euronotes are sometimes underwritten in a manner that guarantees the issuer a specific price. In addition, the underwriters may even guarantee a price at which the notes can be rolled over (reissued at maturity). The Euronotes described here differ from the traditional meaning of medium-term loans provided by Eurobanks.

Euro-Commercial Paper

Euro-commercial paper (Euro-CP) is issued without the backing of a banking syndicate. Maturities can be tailored to satisfy investors. Dealers that place commercial paper have created a secondary market by being willing to purchase existing Euro-CP before maturity.

The Euro-CP rate is typically between 50 and 100 basis points above LIBOR. Euro-CP is sold by dealers, at a transaction cost ranging between 5 and 10 basis points of the face value. This market is tiny compared to the U.S. commercial paper market. Nevertheless, some non-U.S. companies can more easily place their paper here, where they have a household name.

Performance of Foreign Money Market Securities

The performance of an investment in a foreign money market security is measured by the **effective yield** (yield adjusted for the exchange rate), which is dependent on the (1) yield earned on the money market security in the foreign currency and (2) the exchange rate effect. The yield earned on the money market security (Y_f) is

$$Y_f = \frac{SP_f - PP_f}{PP_f}$$

where SP_f = selling price of the foreign money market security in the foreign currency

PP_f = purchase price of the foreign money market security in the foreign currency

The exchange rate effect (denoted as %ΔS) measures the percentage change in the spot exchange rate (in dollars) from the time the foreign currency was obtained to invest in the foreign money market security until the time the security was sold and the foreign currency was converted into the investor's home currency. Thus, the effective yield is

$$Y_e = (1 + Y_f) \times (1 + \%\Delta S) - 1$$

ILLUSTRATION   A U.S. investor obtains Mexican pesos when the peso is worth $.12 and invests in a one-year money market security that provides a yield (in pesos) of 22 percent. At the end of one year, the investor converts the proceeds from the investment back to dollars at the prevailing spot rate of $.13 per peso. In this example, the peso increased in value by 8.33 percent, or .0833. The effective yield earned by the investor is

$$\begin{aligned}
Y_e &= (1 + Y_f) \times (1 + \%\Delta S) - 1 \\
&= (1.22) \times (1.0833) - 1 \\
&= 32.16\%
\end{aligned}$$

The effective yield exceeds the yield quoted on the foreign currency whenever the currency denominating the foreign investment increases in value over the investment horizon.

To illustrate the potential effects of exchange rate movements, the effective yield for a U.S. investor that invests in British money market securities is shown in Exhibit 6.11.

EXHIBIT 6.11 Comparison of Effective Yields between U.S. and British Money Market Yields for a U.S. Investor

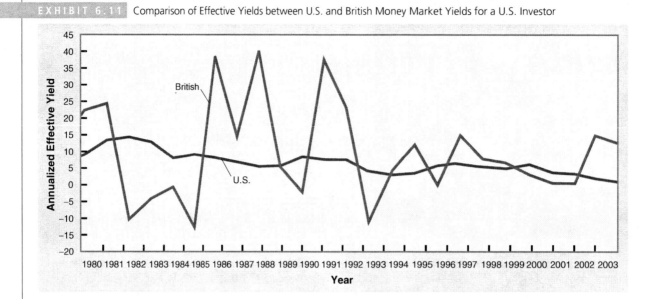

The effective yield was higher than the alternative domestic yields during certain periods as a result of the strengthened pound. Conversely, the effective yield on British money market securities was negative in periods when the pound depreciated. Most investors would not invest in foreign money market securities in every period but would choose to do so only when the foreign currency is expected to appreciate. The results displayed in Exhibit 6.11 show both the high potential yields and the risk from investing in foreign money market securities. The risk could be reduced somewhat by spreading the investment across securities denominated in several currencies.

SUMMARY

■ The main money market securities are Treasury bills, commercial paper, NCDs, repurchase agreements, federal funds, and banker's acceptances. These securities vary according to the issuer. Consequently, their perceived degree of credit risk can vary. They also have different degrees of liquidity. Therefore, the quoted yields at any given point in time vary among money market securities.

■ Financial institutions manage their liquidity by participating in money markets. They may issue money market securities when they experience cash shortages and need to boost liquidity. They can also sell holdings of money market securities to obtain cash.

■ The value of a money market security represents the present value of future cash flows generated by that

security. Since money market securities represent debt, their expected cash flows are typically known. However, the pricing of money market securities changes in response to a shift in the required rate of return by investors. The required rate of return changes in response to interest rate movements or to a shift in the security's credit risk.

■ Interest rates vary among countries. Some investors are attracted to high interest rates in foreign countries, which cause funds to flow to those countries. Consequently, money markets have become globally integrated. Investments in foreign money market securities are subject to exchange rate risk because the foreign currency denominating the securities could depreciate over time.

POINT COUNTER-POINT

Should Firms Invest in Money Market Securities?

Point No. Firms are supposed to use money in a manner that generates an adequate return to shareholders. Money market securities provide a return that is less than that required by shareholders. Thus, firms should not be using shareholder funds to invest in money market securities. If firms need liquidity, they can rely on the money markets for short-term borrowing.

Counter-Point Yes. Firms need money markets for liquidity. If they do not hold any money market securities,

they will frequently be forced to borrow to cover unanticipated cash needs. The lenders may charge higher risk premiums when lending so frequently to these firms.

Who Is Correct? Use InfoTrac or some other source search engine to learn more about this issue. Offer your own opinion on this issue.

QUESTIONS AND APPLICATIONS

1. **Primary Market** Explain how the Treasury uses the primary market to obtain adequate funding.

2. **T-bill Auction** How can investors using the primary T-bill market be assured that their bid will be accepted? Why do large corporations typically make competitive bids rather than noncompetitive bids for T-bills?

3. **Secondary Market for T-bills** Describe the activity in the secondary T-bill market. How can this degree of activity benefit investors in T-bills? Why might a financial institution sometimes consider T-bills as a potential source of funds?

4. **Commercial Paper** Who issues commercial paper? What types of financial institutions issue commercial paper? Why do some firms create a department that can directly place commercial paper? What criteria affect the decision to create such a department?

5. **Commercial Paper Ratings** Why do ratings agencies assign ratings to commercial paper?

6. **Commercial Paper Rates** Explain how investors' preferences for commercial paper change during a recession. How should this reaction affect the difference between commercial paper rates and T-bill rates during recessionary periods?

7. **Negotiable CDs** How can small investors participate in investments in negotiable certificates of deposits (NCDs)?

8. **Repurchase Agreements** Based on what you know about repurchase agreements, would you expect them to have a lower or higher annualized yield than commercial paper? Why?

9. **Banker's Acceptances** Explain how each of the following would use banker's acceptances: (a) exporting firms, (b) importing firms, (c) commercial banks, and (d) investors.

10. **Foreign Money Market Yield** Explain how the yield on a foreign money market security would be affected if the foreign currency denominating that security declines to a greater degree.

11. **Motive to Issue Commercial Paper** The maximum maturity of commercial paper is 270 days. Why would a firm issue commercial paper instead of longer-term securities, even if it needs funds for a long period of time?

12. **Risk and Return of Commercial Paper** You have the choice of investing in top-rated commercial paper or commercial paper that has a lower risk rating. How do you think the risk and return performances of the two investments differ?

13. **Commercial Paper Yield Curve** How do you think the shape of the yield curve for commercial paper and other money market instruments compares to the yield curve for Treasury securities? Explain your logic.

ADVANCED QUESTIONS

14. **Influence of Money Market Activity on Working Capital** Assume that interest rates for most maturities are unusually high. Also, assume that the net working capital (defined as current assets minus current liabilities) levels of many corporations are relatively low in this period. Explain how the money markets

play a role in the relationship between the interest rates and the level of net working capital.

15. **Applying Term Structure Theories to Commercial Paper** Apply the term structure of interest rate theories that were discussed in Chapter 3 to explain the shape of the existing commercial paper yield curve.

INTERPRETING FINANCIAL NEWS

Interpret the following statements made by Wall Street analysts and portfolio managers.

a. "Money markets are not used to get rich, but to avoid being poor."

b. "Until conditions are more favorable, investors are staying on the sidelines."

c. "My portfolio is overinvested in stocks because of the low money market rates."

INTERNET EXERCISE

Go to http://research.stlouisfed.org/fred2. Under "Categories," select "Interest rates." Compare the yield offered on a T-bill to the yield offered by another money market security with a similar maturity. What is the difference in yields? Why do you think the yields differ?

MANAGING IN FINANCIAL MARKETS

Money Market Portfolio Dilemma As the treasurer of a corporation, one of your jobs is to maintain investments in liquid securities such as Treasury securities and commercial paper. Your goal is to earn as high a return as possible but without taking much of a risk.

a. The yield curve is currently upward sloping, such that 10-year Treasury bonds have an annualized yield 3 percentage points above the annualized yield of three-month T-bills. Should you consider using some of your funds to invest in 10-year Treasury securities?

b. Assume that you have substantially more cash than you would possibly need for any liquidity problems. Your boss suggests that you consider investing the excess funds in some money market securities that have a higher return than short-term Treasury securities, such as negotiable certificates of deposit (NCDs). Even though NCDs are less liquid, this would not cause a problem if you have more funds than you need. Given the situation, what use of the excess funds would benefit the firm the most?

c. Assume that commercial paper is currently offering an annualized yield of 7.5 percent, while Treasury securities are offering an annualized yield of 7 percent. Economic conditions have been stable, and you expect conditions to be very favorable over the next six months. Given this situation, would you prefer to hold a diversified portfolio of commercial paper issued by various corporations or T-bills?

d. Assume that commercial paper typically offers a premium of 0.5 percent above the T-bill rate. Given that your firm typically maintains about $10 million in liquid funds, how much extra will you generate per year by investing in commercial paper versus T-bills? Is this extra return worth the risk that the commercial paper could default?

PROBLEMS

1. **T-bill Yield** Assume an investor purchased a six-month T-bill with a $10,000 par value for $9,000 and sold it 90 days later for $9,100. What is the yield?

2. **T-bill Discount** Newly issued three-month T-bills with a par value of $10,000 sold for $9,700. Compute the T-bill discount.

3. **Commercial Paper Yield** Assume an investor purchased six-month commercial paper with a face value of $1 million for $940,000. What is the yield?

4. **Repurchase Agreement** Stanford Corporation arranged a repurchase agreement in which it purchased securities for $4.9 million and will sell the

securities back for $5 million in 40 days. What is the yield (or repo rate) to Stanford Corporation?

5. **T-bill Yield** You paid $98,000 for a $100,000 T-bill maturing in 120 days. If you hold it until maturity, what is the T-bill yield? What is the T-bill discount?

6. **T-bill Yield** The Treasury is selling 91-day T-bills with a face value of $10,000 for $8,800. If the investor holds them until maturity, calculate the yield.

7. **Required Rate of Return** A money market security that has a par value of $10,000 sells for $8,816.60. Given that the security has a maturity of two years, what is the investor's required rate of return?

8. **Effective Yield** A U.S. investor obtains British pounds when the pound is worth $1.50 and invests in a one-year money market security that provides a yield of 5 percent (in pounds). At the end of one year, the investor converts the proceeds from the investment back to dollars at the prevailing spot rate of $1.52 per pound. Calculate the effective yield.

9. **T-bill Yield**
   a. Determine how the annualized yield of a T-bill would be affected if the purchase price is lower. Explain the logic of this relationship.
   b. Determine how the annualized yield of a T-bill would be affected if the selling price is lower. Explain the logic of this relationship.
   c. Determine how the annualized yield of a T-bill would be affected if the number of days is shorter, holding the purchase price and selling price constant. Explain the logic of this relationship.

10. **Return on NCDs** Phil purchased an NCD a year ago in the secondary market for $980,000. The NCD matures today at a price of $1,000,000, and Phil received $45,000 in interest. What is Phil's return on the NCD?

11. **Return on T-bills** Current T-bill yields are approximately 2 percent. Assume an investor considering the purchase of a newly issued three-month T-bill expects interest rates to increase within the next three months and has a required rate of return of 2.5 percent. Based on this information, how much is this investor willing to pay for a three-month T-bill?

FLOW OF FUNDS EXERCISE

Financing in the Money Markets

Recall that Carson Company has obtained substantial loans from finance companies and commercial banks. The interest rate on the loans is tied to market interest rates and is adjusted every six months. It has a credit line with a bank in case it suddenly needs to obtain funds for a temporary period. It previously purchased Treasury securities that it could sell if it experiences any liquidity problems.

If the economy continues to be strong, Carson may need to increase its production capacity by about 50 percent over the next few years to satisfy demand. It is concerned about a possible slowing of the economy because of potential Fed actions to reduce inflation. It needs funding to cover payments for supplies. It is also considering the issuance of stock or bonds to raise funds in the next year.

a. The prevailing commercial paper rate on paper issued by large publicly traded firms is lower than the rate Carson would pay when using a line of credit. Do you think that Carson could issue commercial paper at this prevailing market rate?

b. Should Carson obtain funds to cover payments for supplies by selling its holdings of Treasury securities or by using its credit line? Which alternative has a lower cost? Explain.

WSJ EXERCISE

Assessing Yield Differentials of Money Market Securities

Use the "Money Rates" section of *The Wall Street Journal* to determine the 30-day yield (annualized) of commercial paper, certificates of deposit, banker's acceptances, and T-bills. Which of these securities has the highest yield? Why? Which of these securities has the lowest yield? Why?

5

Bond Markets

B ond markets facilitate the flow of long-term debt from surplus units to deficit units.

The specific objectives of this chapter are to:

■ provide a background on bonds,

■ explain how bond markets are used by institutional investors, and

■ explain how bond markets have become globally integrated.

Background on Bonds

Bonds represent long-term debt securities that are issued by government agencies or corporations. The issuer of a bond is obligated to pay interest (or coupon) payments periodically (such as annually or semiannually) and the par value (principal) at maturity. Bonds are often classified according to the type of issuer. Treasury bonds are issued by the Treasury, federal agency bonds are issued by federal agencies, municipal bonds are issued by state and local governments, and corporate bonds are issued by corporations.

Most bonds have maturities of between 10 and 30 years. Bonds are classified by the ownership structure as either bearer bonds or registered bonds. **Bearer bonds** require the owner to clip coupons attached to the bonds and send them to the issuer to receive coupon payments. **Registered bonds** require the issuer to maintain records of who owns the bond and automatically send coupon payments to the owners.

Bond Yields

The issuer's cost of financing with bonds is commonly measured by the so-called **yield to maturity,** which reflects the annualized yield that is paid by the issuer over the life of the bond. The yield to maturity is the annualized discount rate that equates the future coupon and principal payments to the initial proceeds received from the bond offering.

ILLUSTRATION   Consider an investor who can purchase bonds with 10 years until maturity, a par value of $1,000, and an 8 percent annualized coupon rate for $936. The yield to maturity on this bond can be determined by using a financial calculator as follows:

Input	10	−936	80	1000		
Function Key	N	PV	PMT	FV	CPT	I
Answer						9%

The yield to maturity does not include transaction costs associated with issuing the bond.

An investor who invests in a bond when it is issued and holds it until maturity will earn the yield to maturity. Many investors, however, do not hold a bond to maturity and therefore focus on their holding period return, or the return from their investment over a particular holding period. If they hold the bond for a very short time period (such as less than one year), they may estimate their holding period return as the sum of the coupon payments plus the difference between the selling price and the purchase price of the bond, as a percentage of the purchase price. For relatively long holding periods, a better approximation of the holding period yield is the annualized discount rate that equates the payments received to the initial investment. Since the selling price to be received by investors is uncertain if they do not hold the bond to maturity, their holding period yield is uncertain at the time they purchase the bond. Consequently, an investment in bonds is subject to the risk that the holding period return will be less than expected. The valuation and return of bonds from the investor's perspective are discussed more thoroughly in the following chapter.

http://money.cnn.com/ markets/bondcenter Yields and information on all types of bonds for various maturities.

Treasury and Federal Agency Bonds

The U.S. Treasury commonly issues Treasury notes or Treasury bonds to finance federal government expenditures. The minimum denomination for Treasury notes or bonds is $1,000. The key difference between a note and a bond is that note maturities are usually less than 10 years, whereas bond maturities are 10 years or more. An active over-the-counter secondary market allows investors to sell Treasury notes or bonds prior to maturity.

The yield from holding a Treasury bond, as with other bonds, depends on the coupon rate and on the difference between the purchase price and the selling price. Investors in Treasury notes and bonds receive semiannual interest payments from the Treasury. Although the interest is taxed by the federal government as ordinary income, it is exempt from state and local taxes, if any exist. Domestic and foreign firms and individuals are common investors in Treasury notes and bonds.

Since October 2001, the Treasury has relied on 10-year Treasury bonds to finance the U.S. budget deficit instead of also issuing 30-year Treasury bonds, as it had done previously. Consequently, the Treasury's influence on yields offered on other types of bonds with maturities of 30 years has been reduced.

Treasury Bond Auction

The Treasury obtains long-term funding through Treasury bond offerings, which are conducted through periodic auctions. Treasury bond auctions are normally held in the middle of each quarter. The Treasury announces its plans for an auction, including the date, the amount of funding that it needs, and the maturity of the bonds to be issued. At the time of the auction, financial institutions submit bids for their own accounts or for their clients.

Bids can be submitted on a competitive or a noncompetitive basis. Competitive bids specify a price that the bidder is willing to pay and a dollar amount of securities to be purchased. Noncompetitive bids specify only a dollar amount of securities to be purchased (subject to a maximum limit). The Treasury ranks the competitive bids in descending order according to the price bid per $100 of par value. All competitive bids are accepted until the point at which the desired amount of funding is achieved. Since November 1998, the Treasury has used the lowest accepted bid price as the price applied to all accepted competitive bids and all noncompetitive bids. Competitive bids are commonly used because many bidders want to purchase more Treasury bonds than the maximum that can be purchased on a noncompetitive basis.

The Salomon Brothers Scandal During each Treasury bond offering, bond dealers purchase Treasury bonds and then redistribute them to clients (other financial institutions) that wish to purchase them. During a 1990 Treasury bond auction, Salomon Brothers (now Salomon Smith Barney, a division of Citigroup) purchased 65 percent of the bonds issued, exceeding the 35 percent maximum allowed for any single bond dealer. Some other bond dealers had made commitments to sell Treasury bonds to their clients (financial institutions), but were unable to obtain a sufficient amount because Salomon Brothers had dominated the auction. The other dealers had to obtain the Treasury bonds from Salomon in order to fulfill their commitments. Because Salomon controlled most of the auction, it was able to charge high prices for the bonds desired by the other dealers.

The episode aroused concern that investors might lose faith in the auction process and be discouraged from obtaining Treasury bonds. If the market came to perceive that bond prices were being manipulated, the demand for Treasury bonds would decline, raising the yields that the Treasury would have to offer to sell the bonds and ultimately increasing the cost to taxpayers.

In the summer of 1991, the Securities and Exchange Commission (SEC) and the Justice Department reviewed Salomon Brothers' involvement in the Treasury auction process. On August 18, 1991, the Treasury Department temporarily barred Salomon Brothers from bidding on Treasury securities for clients. In May 1992, Salomon paid fines of $190 million to the SEC and Justice Department. It also created a reserve fund of $100 million to cover claims from civil lawsuits.

Trading Treasury Bonds

Bond dealers serve as intermediaries in the secondary market by matching up buyers and sellers of Treasury bonds, and they also take positions in these bonds. About 2,000 brokers and dealers are registered to trade Treasury securities, but about 30 so-called primary dealers dominate the trading. These dealers make the secondary market for the Treasury bonds. They quote a bid price for customers who want to sell existing Treasury bonds to the dealers and an ask price for customers who want to buy existing Treasury bonds from them. The dealers profit from the spread between the bid and ask prices. Because of the large volume of secondary market transactions and intense competition among bond dealers, the spread is very narrow. When the Federal Reserve engages in open market operations, it normally conducts trading with the primary dealers of government securities. The primary dealers also trade Treasury bonds among themselves.

Treasury bonds are registered at the New York Stock Exchange, but the secondary market trading occurs over-the-counter (through a telecommunications network). The typical daily transaction volume in government securities (including money market securities) for the primary dealers is about $200 billion. Most of this trading volume occurs in the United States, but Treasury bonds are traded worldwide. They are traded in Tokyo from 7:30 P.M. to 3:00 A.M. New York time. The Tokyo and London markets overlap for part of the time, and the London market remains open until 7:30 A.M., when trading begins in New York.

Investors can contact their broker to buy or sell Treasury bonds. The brokerage firms serve as an intermediary between the investors and the bond dealers. Discount brokers usually charge a fee between $40 and $70 for Treasury bond transactions valued at $10,000. Institutional investors tend to contact the bond dealers directly.

Online Trading Investors can also buy bonds through the Treasury-Direct program (http://www.publicdebt.treas.gov). They can have the Treasury deduct their purchase from their bank account. They can also reinvest proceeds received when Treasury bonds mature into newly issued Treasury bonds.

Treasury Bond Quotations

Quotations for Treasury bond prices are published in financial newspapers such as *The Wall Street Journal, Barron's*, and *Investor's Business Daily*. They are also provided in *USA Today* and local newspapers. A typical format for Treasury bond quotations is shown in Exhibit 7.1. Each row represents a specific bond. The coupon rate, shown in the first column, will vary substantially among bonds because bonds issued when interest rates were high (such as in the early 1980s) will have higher coupon rates than those issued when interest rates were low (such as in the 2002–2004 period).

The Treasury bonds are organized in the table according to their maturity (shown in the second column), with those closest to maturity listed first. This allows investors to easily find Treasury bonds that have a specific maturity. If the bond contains a call feature allowing the issuer to repurchase the bonds prior to maturity, it is specified beside the maturity date in the second column. For example, the second and third bonds in Exhibit 7.1 mature in the year 2018 but can be called from the year 2013 on.

The bid price (what a bond dealer is willing to pay) and the ask price (what a bond dealer is willing to sell the bond for) are quoted per hundreds of dollars of par value, with fractions (to the right of the colon) expressed as thirty-seconds of a dollar. For example, if the first bond has a face value of $100,000, its ask price will be $120,719. This bond has a much higher price than the other two bonds shown, primarily because it offers a higher coupon rate. However, its yield to maturity is similar to the other yields (see the last column in Exhibit 7.1). From an investor's point of view, the coupon rate advantage over the other two bonds is essentially offset by the high price to be paid for that bond.

Online Quotations Treasury bond prices are accessible online at http://www.investingin bonds.com. This website provides the spread between the bid and the ask (offer) prices for various maturities. Treasury bond yields are accessible online at http://www.federalre serve.gov/releases/H15/. The yields are updated on a daily basis and are disclosed for several different maturities.

EXHIBIT 7.1

Example of Bond Price Quotations

Rate	Maturity Date	Bid	Ask	Yield
10.75	Aug. 2005	120:17	120:23	8.37%
8.38	Aug. 2013–18	100:09	100:15	8.32%
8.75	Nov. 2013–18	103:05	103:11	8.34%

WSJ

Government Bond Price Quotations

Government bond price quotations in the secondary market are reported in *The Wall Street Journal,* as shown here. The table is organized by term to maturity; bonds that have the shortest term to maturity are listed first. For each bond, the coupon rate is shown in the first column, the maturity date in the second column, the bid price (per $100 of par value) in the third column, and the ask price (per $100 of par value) in the fourth column. The bid and ask price quotations after the colon are in thirty-seconds, so a quote of 100:03 reflects a

price of $100.09 per $100 of par value. The change in the bond's price from the previous day in thirty-seconds is shown in the fifth column, so a change of 1 reflects an increase of $\frac{1}{32}$, or $.03125 per $100 of par value. Notice that the changes in prices are much larger for bonds with longer terms to maturity. The yield to maturity is listed in the last column for investors who plan to purchase bonds today and hold them to maturity. The yield curve can be derived by plotting the yield to maturity for various maturities shown in the last column.

TREASURY BONDS, NOTES & BILLS

Explanatory Notes

Representative Over-the-Counter quotation based on transactions of $1 million or more. Treasury bond, note and bill quotes are as of mid-afternoon. Colons in bid-and-asked quotes represent 32nds; 101:01 means 101 1/32. Net changes in 32nds. n-Treasury note. i-Inflation-Indexed issue. Treasury bill quotes in hundredths, quoted on terms of a rate of discount. Days to maturity calculated from settlement date. All yields are to maturity and based on the asked quote. Latest 13-week and 26-week bills are boldfaced. For bonds callable prior to maturity, yields are computed to the earliest call date for issues quoted above par and to the maturity date for issues below par. *When issued.

Source: eSpeed/Cantor Fitzgerald

U.S. Treasury strips as of 3 p.m. Eastern time, also based on transactions of $1 million or more. Colons in bid and asked quotes represent 32nds; 99:01 means 99 1/32. Net changes in 32nds. Yields calculated on the asked quotation. ci-stripped coupon interest. bp-Treasury bond, stripped principal. np-Treasury note, stripped principal. For bonds callable prior to maturity, yields are computed to the earliest call date for issues quoted above par and to the maturity date for issues below par.

Source: Bear, Stearns & Co. via Street Software Technology Inc.

RATE	MATURITY MO/YR	BID	ASKED	CHG	ASK YLD
3.500	Jan 11i	112:29	112:30	-6	1.39
5.000	Feb 11n	107:00	107:00	-6	3.78
13.875	May 11	120:01	120:02	...	2.20
5.000	Aug 11n	106:27	106:28	-7	3.87
14.000	Nov 11	125:11	125:12	-2	2.41
3.375	Jan 12i	112:24	112:25	-6	1.55
4.875	Feb 12n	105:26	105:27	-7	3.97
3.000	Jul 12i	110:00	110:01	-6	1.65
4.375	Aug 12n	102:07	102:08	-7	4.04
4.000	Nov 12n	99:17	99:18	-7	4.06
10.375	Nov 12	122:24	122:25	-5	2.99
3.875	Feb 13n	98:11	98:12	-7	4.10
3.625	May 13n	96:12	96:13	-6	4.11
1.875	Jul 13i	100:27	100:28	-7	1.77
4.250	Aug 13n	100:13	100:14	-8	4.19
12.000	Aug 13	133:01	133:02	-2	3.16
4.250	Nov 13n	100:07	100:08	-7	4.22
2.000	Jan 14i	101:20	101:21	-7	1.81
4.000	Feb 14n	98:04	98:05	-8	4.24
4.750	May 14n	103:30	103:31	-8	4.25
13.250	May 14	143:00	143:01	-5	3.39
2.000	Jul 14i	101:12	101:13	-7	1.84
12.500	Aug 14	141:06	141:07	-7	3.47
11.750	Nov 14	139:02	139:03	-6	3.54
11.250	Feb 15	158:03	158:04	-12	4.31
10.625	Aug 15	154:03	154:04	-11	4.38
9.875	Nov 15	147:28	147:29	-11	4.42
9.250	Feb 16	142:20	142:21	-11	4.47
7.250	May 16	124:16	124:17	-10	4.54
7.500	Nov 16	127:01	127:02	-10	4.59
8.750	May 17	139:19	139:20	-11	4.61
8.875	Aug 17	141:04	141:05	-11	4.63
9.125	May 18	144:18	144:19	-11	4.69
9.000	Nov 18	143:25	143:26	-13	4.74
8.875	Feb 19	142:20	142:21	-13	4.77
8.125	Aug 19	135:02	135:03	-11	4.81
8.500	Feb 20	139:19	139:20	-9	4.84
8.750	May 20	142:22	142:23	-9	4.84
8.750	Aug 20	142:28	142:29	-9	4.86
7.875	Feb 21	133:07	133:08	-8	4.91
8.125	May 21	136:10	136:11	-8	4.91
8.125	Aug 21	136:16	136:17	-9	4.93
8.000	Nov 21	135:07	135:08	-9	4.94
7.250	Aug 22	126:17	126:18	-8	5.00
7.625	Nov 22	131:09	131:10	-8	4.99
7.125	Feb 23	125:07	125:08	-8	5.02
6.250	Aug 23	114:16	114:17	-8	5.05
7.500	Nov 24	130:29	130:30	-8	5.04
2.375	Jan 25i	102:07	102:08	-5	2.24
7.625	Feb 25	132:19	132:20	-9	5.05
6.875	Aug 25	123:01	123:02	-8	5.08
6.000	Feb 26	111:19	111:20	-7	5.10
6.750	Aug 26	121:20	121:21	-8	5.10
6.500	Nov 26	118:11	118:12	-9	5.11
6.625	Feb 27	120:02	120:03	-8	5.11
6.375	Aug 27	116:27	116:28	-7	5.12
6.125	Nov 27	113:16	113:17	-7	5.12
3.625	Apr 28i	124:10	124:11	-4	2.29
5.500	Aug 28	105:00	105:01	-7	5.13
5.250	Nov 28	101:19	101:20	-7	5.13

RATE	MATURITY MO/YR	BID	ASKED	CHG	ASK YLD
Government Bonds & Notes					
6.000	Aug 04n	100:02	100:03	...	1.13
7.250	Aug 04n	100:02	100:03	...	1.51
13.750	Aug 04	100:05	100:06	-1	0.63
2.125	Aug 04n	100:01	100:02	...	1.02
1.875	Sep 04n	100:02	100:03	...	1.19
2.125	Oct 04n	100:04	100:05	...	1.41
5.875	Nov 04n	101:04	101:05	...	1.39
7.875	Nov 04n	101:21	101:22	...	1.42
11.625	Nov 04	102:20	102:21	-1	1.41
2.000	Nov 04n	100:04	100:05	...	1.48
1.750	Dec 04n	100:01	100:02	...	1.54
1.625	Jan 05n	100:00	100:00	...	1.62
7.500	Feb 05n	102:29	102:30	-2	1.70
1.500	Feb 05n	99:28	99:29	-1	1.64
1.625	Mar 05n	99:29	99:30	-1	1.72
1.625	Apr 05n	99:28	99:29	-1	1.75
6.500	May 05n	103:16	103:17	-2	1.80
6.750	May 05n	103:22	103:23	-2	1.82
12.000	May 05	107:23	107:24	-1	1.73
1.250	May 05n	99:17	99:18	-2	1.80
1.125	Jun 05n	99:11	99:12	-1	1.84
1.500	Jul 05n	99:19	99:20	-1	1.89
6.500	Aug 05n	104:18	104:19	-3	1.89
10.750	Aug 05	108:26	108:27	-2	1.90
2.000	Aug 05n	100:02	100:03	-2	1.91
1.625	Sep 05n	99:19	99:20	-2	1.94
1.625	Oct 05n	99:16	99:17	-2	2.00
5.750	Nov 05n	104:18	104:19	-3	2.03
5.875	Nov 05n	104:23	104:24	-3	2.03
1.875	Nov 05n	99:23	99:24	-3	2.06
1.875	Dec 05n	99:20	99:21	-3	2.12
1.875	Jan 06n	99:18	99:19	-3	2.16
5.625	Feb 06n	105:05	105:06	-3	2.11
9.375	Feb 06	110:22	110:23	-3	2.13
1.625	Feb 06n	99:03	99:04	-3	2.19
1.500	Mar 06n	98:25	98:26	-3	2.23
2.250	Apr 06n	99:28	99:29	-4	2.30
2.000	May 06n	99:15	99:16	-2	2.29
4.625	May 06n	103:30	103:31	-3	2.30
6.875	May 06n	107:26	107:27	-3	2.30
2.500	May 06n	100:08	100:09	-3	2.34
2.750	Jun 06n	100:21	100:22	-3	2.37

RATE	MATURITY MO/YR	BID	ASKED	CHG	ASK YLD
7.000	Jul 06n	108:19	108:20	-3	2.40
2.750	Jul 06n	100:18	100:19	-4	2.43
2.375	Aug 06n	99:27	99:28	-3	2.43
6.500	Oct 06n	108:11	108:12	-4	2.53
2.625	Nov 06n	100:04	100:05	-3	2.55
3.500	Nov 06n	102:01	102:02	-3	2.55
3.375	Jan 07i	107:15	107:16	-2	0.28
2.250	Feb 07n	99:00	99:01	-4	2.64
6.250	Feb 07n	108:22	108:23	-3	2.64
6.625	May 07n	110:06	110:07	-4	2.75
4.375	May 07n	104:08	104:09	-4	2.75
3.125	May 07n	100:30	100:31	-4	2.75
3.250	Aug 07n	101:05	101:06	-4	2.83
6.125	Aug 07n	109:11	109:12	-5	2.85
3.000	Nov 07n	100:08	100:09	-4	2.91
3.625	Jan 08i	110:01	110:02	-4	0.65
3.000	Feb 08n	100:00	100:00	-5	3.00
5.500	Feb 08n	108:08	108:09	-5	2.99
2.625	May 08n	98:11	98:12	-4	3.08
5.625	May 08n	108:29	108:30	-5	3.09
3.250	Aug 08n	100:08	100:09	-5	3.17
3.125	Sep 08n	99:22	99:23	-5	3.19
3.125	Oct 08n	99:19	99:20	-5	3.22
3.375	Nov 08n	100:16	100:17	-5	3.24
4.750	Nov 08n	106:00	106:00	-5	3.23
3.375	Dec 08n	100:13	100:14	-5	3.27
3.250	Jan 09n	99:25	99:26	-5	3.30
3.875	Jan 09i	112:20	112:21	-5	0.95
3.000	Feb 09n	98:20	98:21	-5	3.32
2.625	Mar 09n	96:30	96:31	-5	3.34
3.125	Apr 09n	98:29	98:30	-6	3.37
3.875	May 09n	102:03	102:04	-6	3.38
5.500	May 09n	109:12	109:13	-6	3.34
4.000	Jun 09n	102:19	102:20	-6	3.40
3.625	Jul 09n	100:28	100:29	-6	3.42
6.000	Aug 09n	111:21	111:22	-7	3.44
10.375	Nov 09	102:13	102:14	...	1.02
4.250	Jan 10i	116:01	116:02	-6	1.19
6.500	Feb 10n	114:19	114:20	-6	3.56
11.750	Feb 10	105:06	105:07	1	1.51
10.000	May 10	106:08	106:09	1	1.66
5.750	Aug 10n	111:04	111:05	-6	3.67
12.750	Nov 10	113:08	113:09	1	2.03

Stripped Treasury Bonds

The cash flows of bonds are commonly transformed (stripped) by securities firms so that one security represents the principal payment only while a second security represents the interest payments. For example, consider a 10-year Treasury bond with a par value of $100,000 that has a 12 percent coupon rate and semiannual coupon payments. This bond could be stripped into a principal-only (PO) security that will provide $100,000 upon maturity and an interest-only (IO) security that will provide 20 semiannual payments of $6,000 each.

Investors who desire a lump-sum payment in the distant future can choose the PO part, and investors desiring periodic cash inflows can select the IO part. Because the cash flows of the underlying securities are different, so are the degrees of interest rate sensitivity.

A market for Treasury strips was originally created by securities firms in the early 1980s. Merrill Lynch created the Treasury Investment Growth Receipts (TIGRs) by purchasing Treasury securities and then stripping them to create PO and IO securities. Other securities firms also began to create their own versions of these **stripped securities.** In 1985, the Treasury created the STRIPS program, which exchanges stripped securities for underlying Treasury securities. STRIPS are not issued by the Treasury, but are created and sold by various financial institutions. They can be created for any Treasury security. Since they are components of Treasury securities, they are backed by the U.S. government. They do not have to be held until maturity, as there is an active secondary market. STRIPS have become very popular. More than $11 billion of securites are being stripped every month.

Inflation-Indexed Treasury Bonds

In 1996, the Treasury announced that it would periodically issue inflation-indexed bonds that provide returns tied to the inflation rate. These bonds, commonly referred to as TIPS (Treasury inflation-protected securities), are intended for investors who wish to ensure that the returns on their investments keep up with the increase in prices over time. The coupon rate offered on TIPS is lower than the rate on typical Treasury bonds, but the principal value is increased by the amount of the U.S. inflation rate (as measured by the percentage increase in the consumer price index) every six months.

ILLUSTRATION Consider a 10-year inflation-indexed bond that has a par value of $10,000 and a coupon rate of 4 percent. Assume that during the first six months since the bond was issued, the inflation rate (as measured by the consumer price index) was 1 percent. The principal of the bond is increased by $100 (1% × $10,000). Thus, the coupon payment after six months will be 2 percent (half of the yearly coupon rate) of the new par value, or 2% × $10,100 = $202. Assume that the inflation rate over the next six months is 3 percent. The principal of the bond is increased by $303 (3% × $10,100), which results in a new par value of $10,403. The coupon payment at the end of the year is based on the coupon rate and the new par value, or 2% × $10,403 = $208.06. This process is applied every six months over the life of the bond. If prices double over the 10-year period in which the bond exists, the par value of the bond will also double and thus will be equal to $20,000 at maturity.

Inflation-indexed government bonds have become very popular in some other countries where inflation tends to be high, including Australia, Turkey, Brazil, and the United Kingdom. They are also becoming popular in the United States.

Savings Bonds

Savings bonds are issued by the Treasury, but can be purchased from many financial institutions. They are attractive to small investors because they can be purchased with as little as $25. Larger denominations are available as well. The Series EE savings bond provides a market-based rate of interest, while the I savings bond provides a rate of interest that is tied to inflation. The interest accumulates monthly and adds value to the amount received at the time of redemption.

Savings bonds have a 30-year maturity and do not have a secondary market. The Treasury does allow savings bonds issued after February 2003 to be redeemed anytime after a 12-month period, but there is a penalty equal to the last three months of interest.

The interest income on savings bonds is not subject to state and local taxes, but is subject to federal taxes. For federal tax purposes, investors holding savings bonds can report the accumulated interest on an annual basis or only at the time they redeem the bonds or at maturity.

Federal Agency Bonds

Federal agency bonds are issued by federal agencies. The **Government National Mortgage Association (Ginnie Mae)** issues bonds and uses the proceeds to purchase mortgages that are insured by the Federal Housing Administration (FHA) and by the Veteran's Administration (VA). The bonds are backed both by the mortgages that are purchased with the proceeds and by the federal government.

The Federal Home Loan Mortgage Association (called Freddie Mac) issues bonds and uses the proceeds to purchase conventional mortgages. These bonds are not backed by the federal government, but have a very low degree of credit risk.

The **Federal National Mortgage Association (Fannie Mae)** is a federally chartered corporation owned by individual investors. It issues bonds and uses the proceeds to purchase residential mortgages. These bonds are not backed by the federal government, but have a very low degree of credit risk.

Municipal Bonds

Like the federal government, state and local governments frequently spend more than the revenues they receive. To finance the difference, they issue **municipal bonds,** most of which can be classified as either **general obligation bonds** or **revenue bonds.** Payments on general obligation bonds are supported by the municipal government's ability to tax, whereas payments on revenue bonds must be generated by revenues of the project (tollway, toll bridge, state college dormitory, etc.) for which the bonds were issued.

The volume of state and local government bonds issued is displayed in Exhibit 7.2. Revenue bonds have generally dominated since 1975. The total amount of bond financing by state and local governments has generally increased over time.

Credit Risk

Both types of municipal bonds are subject to some degree of credit (default) risk. If a municipality is unable to increase taxes, it could default on general obligation bonds. If it issues revenue bonds and does not generate sufficient revenue, it could default on these bonds.

Government Agency & Similar Issues

Bond price quotations provided for bonds issued by Fannie Mae, Freddie Mac, and other government agencies are disclosed in *The Wall Street Journal*. The coupon rate is provided in the first column, while the maturity date is in the second column. The bid and ask prices are quoted in the third and fourth columns, while the yield to maturity is disclosed in the fifth column.

Government Agency & Similar Issues

Over-the-Counter mid-afternoon quotations based on large transactions, usually $1 million or more. Colons in bid and asked quotes represent 32nds; 101:01 means 101 1/32.

All yields are calculated to maturity, and based on the asked quote.

*Callable issue, maturity date shown. For issues callable prior to maturity, yields are computed to the earliest call date for issues quoted above par, or 100, and to the maturity date for issues below par.

Source: Bear, Stearns & Co. via Street Software Technology Inc.

Fannie Mae Issues

RATE	MAT	BID	ASKED	YLD
6.50	8-04	100:02	100:04	...
3.50	9-04	100:06	100:08	0.98
1.88	12-04	100:00	100:02	1.71
7.13	2-05	102:20	102:22	1.82
3.88	3-05	101:03	101:05	1.89
5.75	6-05	103:00	103:02	2.08
7.00	7-05	104:13	104:15	2.12
1.88	9-05	99:26	99:28	2.00
2.88	10-05	100:29	100:31	2.03
6.00	12-05	105:00	105:02	2.15
2.00	1-06	99:18	99:20	2.26
5.50	2-06	104:20	104:22	2.32
2.13	4-06	99:15	99:17	2.41
5.50	5-06	104:29	104:31	2.54
2.25	5-06	99:17	99:19	2.49
5.25	6-06	104:26	104:28	2.52
2.50	6-06	99:29	99:31	2.52
1.75	6-06	98:11	98:13	2.64
2.75	8-06	99:29	99:31	2.77
4.38	10-06	103:15	103:17	2.70
2.63	11-06	99:21	99:23	2.76
4.75	1-07	104:03	104:05	2.94
5.00	1-07	104:31	105:01	2.84
2.63	1-07*	99:03	99:05	2.98
2.38	2-07	98:22	98:24	2.89
7.13	3-07	109:28	109:30	3.11
5.25	4-07	105:25	105:26	2.97
4.25	7-07	103:07	103:09	3.07
6.63	10-07	110:09	110:11	3.18
3.50	10-07*	101:03	101:05	...
3.25	11-07	100:04	100:06	3.19
3.25	1-08	99:27	99:29	3.28
3.50	1-08*	100:08	100:10	2.83
5.75	2-08	107:31	108:01	3.30
6.00	5-08	109:04	109:04	3.39
2.88	5-08*	97:24	97:26	3.50
2.50	6-08	96:23	96:25	3.40
3.25	8-08	99:01	99:03	3.50
4.00	9-08	101:12	101:14	3.62
3.75	9-08*	99:21	99:23	3.83
3.88	11-08*	100:03	100:05	3.74
3.38	12-08	98:30	99:00	3.62
4.00	12-08*	100:15	100:17	3.34
5.25	1-09	106:14	106:16	3.65
3.25	2-09	98:06	98:08	3.67
3.13	3-09*	96:31	97:01	3.84

RATE	MAT	BID	ASKED	YLD
4.25	5-09	102:03	102:05	3.75
6.38	6-09	111:11	111:13	3.78
6.63	9-09	112:20	112:22	3.85
7.25	1-10	115:30	116:00	3.95
7.13	6-10	115:26	115:28	4.05
6.63	11-10	113:17	113:19	4.14
6.25	2-11	110:03	110:05	4.43
5.50	3-11	107:08	107:10	4.22
6.00	5-11	110:00	110:02	4.27
5.50	10-11*	101:27	101:29	...
5.38	11-11	106:04	106:06	4.37
5.00	11-11*	100:05	100:07	4.17
6.00	12-11*	101:15	101:17	1.72
6.00	1-12*	101:24	101:26	1.80
6.13	3-12	110:23	110:25	4.43
6.25	3-12*	102:15	102:17	2.04
5.50	7-12*	101:26	101:28	3.45
5.25	8-12	103:01	103:03	4.78
4.38	9-12	98:31	99:01	4.52
4.75	2-13*	98:23	98:25	4.93
4.63	5-13	98:06	98:08	4.87
4.38	7-13*	96:12	96:14	4.87
4.63	10-13	99:18	99:20	4.68
5.13	1-14	100:27	100:29	5.00
4.13	4-14	95:08	95:10	4.73
6.25	5-29	109:13	109:17	5.54
7.13	1-30	121:01	121:05	5.56
7.25	5-30	122:28	123:00	5.56
6.63	11-30	114:13	114:17	5.57

Freddie Mac

RATE	MAT	BID	ASKED	YLD
4.50	8-04	100:01	100:03	...
3.25	11-04	100:12	100:14	1.59
6.88	1-05	102:03	102:05	1.76
1.88	1-05	99:31	100:01	1.83
3.88	2-05	100:30	101:00	1.88
1.75	5-05	99:22	99:24	2.08
4.25	6-05	101:23	101:25	2.11
7.00	7-05	104:12	104:14	2.13
1.50	8-05	99:17	99:19	1.90
2.88	9-05	100:28	100:30	2.00
2.13	11-05	99:29	99:31	2.15
5.25	1-06	104:03	104:05	2.26
1.88	2-06	99:09	99:11	2.32
2.38	4-06	99:28	99:30	2.41
5.50	7-06	105:14	105:16	2.55
2.75	8-06	100:06	100:08	2.62
2.88	11-06*	99:26	99:28	2.94

RATE	MAT	BID	ASKED	YLD
2.88	12-06	100:04	100:06	2.79
2.38	2-07	98:23	98:25	2.88
4.88	3-07	104:25	104:27	2.92
3.50	9-07	100:31	101:01	3.14
4.00	10-07*	101:17	101:19	...
3.25	2-08*	99:13	99:14	3.41
2.75	3-08	98:03	98:05	3.30
3.50	4-08*	99:18	99:20	3.61
5.75	4-08	108:06	108:09	3.34
3.63	9-08	100:10	100:12	3.53
5.13	10-08	106:03	106:05	3.53
3.88	1-09*	99:25	99:27	3.91
5.75	3-09	108:21	108:23	3.67
3.38	4-09	98:14	98:16	3.72
4.25	7-09	102:00	102:02	3.79
4.75	8-09*	100:02	100:04	...
6.63	9-09	112:22	112:24	3.85
4.38	2-10*	99:30	100:02	4.37
7.00	3-10	114:31	115:01	3.98
6.88	9-10	114:23	114:25	4.11
4.75	12-10*	100:24	100:26	4.11
4.13	2-11*	98:01	98:03	4.46
5.63	3-11	107:31	108:01	4.22
5.88	3-11	108:01	108:03	4.45
6.00	6-11	110:04	110:06	4.27
6.38	8-11*	105:18	105:20	3.40
5.50	9-11	107:00	107:02	4.33
5.75	1-12	108:15	108:17	4.39
6.25	3-12*	105:30	106:00	3.78
5.13	7-12	104:05	104:07	4.49
5.13	8-12*	100:03	100:05	...
4.75	10-12*	99:01	99:03	4.89
5.25	11-12*	101:03	101:05	4.85
4.50	1-13	99:15	99:17	4.57
4.38	3-13	98:16	98:18	4.58
4.75	5-13*	97:19	97:21	5.09
4.00	6-13*	94:09	94:11	4.79
4.50	7-13	98:30	99:00	4.64
5.13	11-13*	100:01	100:03	5.05
4.88	11-13	101:12	101:14	4.68
4.50	1-14	98:12	98:14	4.70
5.00	1-14*	99:15	99:17	5.06
6.75	9-29	115:25	115:29	5.57
6.75	3-31	116:09	116:13	5.56
6.25	7-32	109:24	109:28	5.55

Federal Farm Credit Bank

RATE	MAT	BID	ASKED	YLD
2.38	10-04	100:03	100:05	1.29
3.88	12-04	100:22	100:24	1.70
3.88	2-05	100:28	100:30	1.86
4.38	4-05	101:16	101:18	2.02
2.13	3-06	100:06	100:08	1.89
2.50	11-05	100:13	100:15	2.12
2.63	12-05	100:17	100:19	2.18
2.50	3-06	100:06	100:08	2.34
2.25	9-06	99:02	99:04	2.69

RATE	MAT	BID	ASKED	YLD
2.38	10-06	99:11	99:13	2.66
3.00	4-08*	98:24	98:26	3.35

Federal Home Loan Bank

RATE	MAT	BID	ASKED	YLD
3.63	10-04	100:11	100:13	1.38
4.13	11-04	100:19	100:21	1.59
4.00	2-05	101:00	101:02	1.90
4.38	2-05	101:06	101:08	1.89
1.63	4-05	99:21	99:23	2.02
6.88	8-05	104:27	104:29	1.93
2.25	12-05	100:00	100:02	2.20
2.50	12-05	100:11	100:13	2.20
2.00	2-06	99:14	99:16	2.34
5.13	3-06	103:25	103:27	2.61
2.50	3-06	99:28	99:30	2.53
5.38	5-06	104:27	104:29	2.51
2.25	5-06	99:17	99:19	2.48
1.88	6-06	98:25	98:27	2.51
2.88	9-06	100:12	100:14	2.66
4.88	11-06	104:15	104:17	2.79
1.88	1-07	97:23	97:25	2.83
4.88	2-07	104:20	104:22	2.93
5.38	2-07	105:26	105:28	2.93
2.75	3-08	98:03	98:05	3.30
2.63	7-08	96:29	96:31	3.46
5.80	9-08	108:15	108:17	3.53
3.63	11-08	100:00	100:02	3.61
6.00	5-11	109:17	109:19	4.34
5.63	11-11	107:12	107:14	4.42
5.75	5-12	108:11	108:13	4.46
4.50	11-12	99:19	99:21	4.55
3.88	6-13	94:23	94:25	4.60
4.50	9-13	98:24	98:26	4.66
5.25	6-14	103:26	103:28	4.75

GNMA Mtge. Issues

RATE	MAT	BID	ASKED	YLD
4.00	30Yr	92:14	92:16	5.19
4.50	30Yr	96:07	96:09	5.16
5.00	30Yr	99:05	99:07	5.19
5.50	30Yr	101:17	101:19	5.12
6.00	30Yr	103:16	103:18	4.80
6.50	30Yr	104:31	105:01	4.24
7.00	30Yr	106:14	106:16	3.74
7.50	30Yr	107:20	107:22	3.77
8.00	30Yr	108:25	108:27	3.95
8.50	30Yr	108:31	109:01	4.47

Tennessee Valley Authority

RATE	MAT	BID	ASKED	YLD
6.38	6-05	103:17	103:19	2.04
5.38	11-08	106:15	106:17	3.70
5.63	1-11	107:31	108:02	4.18
6.00	3-13	100:00	100:08	4.58
4.75	8-13	100:29	100:31	4.62
6.25	12-17	111:13	111:16	5.05
6.75	11-25	114:15	114:18	5.57
7.13	5-30	120:28	121:00	5.58

Nevertheless, in general the risk of default on municipal bonds is low. Less than .5 percent of all municipal bonds issued since 1940 have defaulted. Because there is some concern about the risk of default, investors commonly monitor the ratings of municipal bonds. Moody's, Standard & Poor's, and Fitch Investor Service assign ratings to municipal bonds based on the ability of the issuer to repay the debt. The ratings are important to the issuer because a better rating will cause investors to require a smaller risk premium, and the municipal bonds can be issued at a higher price (lower yield).

EXHIBIT 7.2 Dollar Volume of State and Local Government Securities Issued

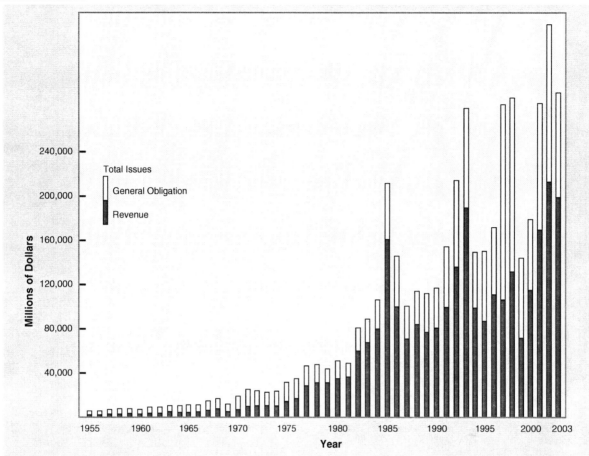

Sources: Bloomberg, L.P.; J. P. Morgan; Salomon Brothers; *Current Issues in Economics and Finance,* FRBNY, June 1995, p. 4, updated by author.

Some municipal bonds are insured to protect against default. The issuer pays for this protection, so that it can issue the bond at a higher price, which translates into a higher price paid by the investor. Thus, investors indirectly bear the cost of the insurance.

Characteristics of Municipal Bonds

Revenue bonds and general obligation bonds typically promise semiannual interest payments. Common purchasers of these bonds include financial and nonfinancial institutions as well as individuals. The minimum denomination of municipal bonds is typically $5,000. A secondary market exists for them, although it is less active than the one for Treasury bonds.

Most municipal bonds contain a call provision, which allows the issuer to repurchase the bonds at a specified price before the bonds mature. A municipality may exercise its option to repurchase the bonds if interest rates decline substantially because it can reissue bonds at the lower interest rate and reduce its cost of financing.

Variable-Rate Municipal Bonds Variable-rate municipal bonds have a floating interest rate based on a benchmark interest rate. The coupon payment adjusts to movements in the benchmark interest rate. Some variable-rate municipal bonds are convertible to a fixed rate until maturity under specified conditions. In general, variable-rate municipal bonds are desirable to investors who expect that interest rates will rise. However, there is the risk that interest rates may decline over time, which would cause the coupon payments to decline as well.

Tax Advantages One of the most attractive features of municipal bonds is that the interest income is normally exempt from federal taxes. Second, the interest income earned on bonds that are issued by a municipality within a particular state is normally exempt from state income taxes (if any). Thus, investors who reside in states that impose income taxes can reduce their taxes further.

Trading and Quotations

Today, there are more than 1 million different bonds outstanding, and more than 50,000 different issuers of municipal bonds. There are hundreds of bond dealers that can accommodate investor requests to buy or sell municipal bonds in the secondary market, but only five dealers account for more than half of all the trading volume. Bond dealers can also take positions in municipal bonds.

Investors who expect that they will not hold a municipal bond until maturity should ensure that the bonds they consider have active secondary market trading. Many of the municipal bonds have an inactive secondary market. Therefore, it is difficult to know the prevailing market values of these bonds. While investors do not pay a direct commission on trades, they incur transactions costs in the form of a bid-ask spread on the bonds. This spread can be large, especially for the municipal bonds that are rarely traded in the secondary market.

The electronic trading of municipal bonds is becoming very popular, in part because it enables investors to circumvent the more expensive route of calling brokers. Trading Edge, a broker of fixed-income securities, established an electronic trading website, http://www.tradingedge.com in 1999. Another popular electronic bond website is http://www.eBondTrade.com. Such websites provide access to information on municipal bonds and allow online buying and selling of municipal bonds.

Municipal bond price quotations are accessible online at http://www.munidirect.com and at http://www.investinginbonds.com. Quotations can be obtained for any state and can be sorted by maturity, credit rating, coupon rate, or other characteristics.

Yields Offered on Municipal Bonds

The yield offered by a municipal bond differs from the yield on a Treasury bond with the same maturity for three reasons. First, the municipal bond must pay a risk premium to compensate for the possibility of default risk. Second, the municipal bond must pay a slight premium to compensate for being less liquid than Treasury bonds with the same maturity. Third, as explained earlier, the income earned from a municipal bond is exempt from federal taxes. This tax advantage of municipal bonds more than offsets their two disadvantages and allows municipal bonds to offer a lower yield than Treasury bonds.

Yield Curve on Municipal Bonds At any given time, there are municipal bonds in the secondary market that have only a short time to maturity and others that have longer terms to maturity. A municipal bond yield curve can be constructed from the municipal bonds that are available. An example of a municipal bond yield curve is shown in

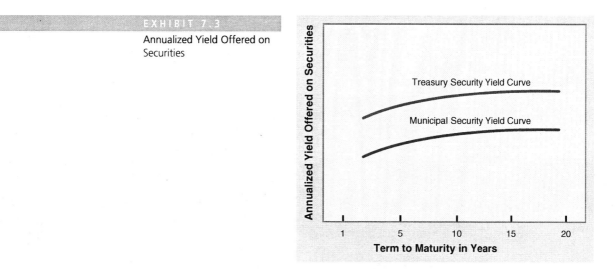

Annualized Yield Offered on Securities

Exhibit 7.3, which also includes a Treasury yield curve for comparison. Notice that the municipal security yield curve is lower than the Treasury yield curve, which is primarily attributed to the tax differential between the two types of securities. The gap due to the tax differential is offset slightly by the default risk and liquidity differential. The yield on municipal securities is commonly 20 to 30 percent less than the yield offered on Treasury securities with similar maturities.

The shape of a municipal security yield curve tends to be similar to the shape of a Treasury security yield curve for two reasons. First, like the Treasury yield curve, the municipal yield curve is influenced by interest rate expectations. If investors expect interest rates to rise, they tend to favor shorter-term securities, which results in high short-term security prices and low short-term yields in both the municipal and Treasury markets. Second, investors require a premium for longer-term securities with lower liquidity in both the municipal and Treasury markets. If supply conditions differ, the shapes could differ.

ILLUSTRATION At a particular point in time, assume that the economy is strong and municipalities experience budget surpluses. Many of them will not have to issue new bonds, so those municipalities that do need long-term funds can more easily find buyers. Meanwhile, the Treasury may still issue new long-term securities to finance the existing federal deficit. In this case, the gap between the Treasury and municipal yields may be larger for new long-term securities than for the securities that were issued in the past and now have a shorter term to maturity.

Corporate Bonds

When corporations need to borrow for long-term periods, they issue **corporate bonds,** which usually promise the owner interest on a semiannual basis. The minimum denomination is $1,000. Larger bond offerings are normally achieved through public offerings, which must first be registered with the SEC. The degree of secondary market activity varies; some big corporations have a large amount of bonds outstanding, which increases secondary market activity and the bonds' liquidity. The bonds issued by smaller corporations tend to be less liquid because their trading volume is relatively low.

Although most corporate bonds have maturities between 10 and 30 years, corporations such as Boeing, Ford, and ChevronTexaco have recently issued 50-year bonds. These bonds can be attractive to insurance companies that are attempting to match their long-term policy obligations. Recently, Bell South, the Coca-Cola Company, and Walt Disney Company issued 100-year bonds.

The interest paid by corporations is tax deductible, which reduces the corporate cost of financing with bonds. Since equity (stock) financing by corporations does not involve interest payments, it does not offer such a tax advantage.

Corporate Bond Yields and Risk

Institutional and individual investors who want an investment that provides stable income may consider purchasing corporate bonds. The interest income earned on corporate bonds represents ordinary income to the bondholders and is therefore subject to federal and state (if any) taxes. Thus, corporate bonds do not provide the same tax benefits to bondholders as municipal bonds.

Yield Curve At a given point in time, the yield curve for corporate bonds will be affected by interest rate expectations, a liquidity premium, and the specific maturity preferences of corporations issuing bonds. Since these are the same factors that affect the yield curve of Treasury bonds, the shape of the yield curve for corporate bonds will also normally be similar to the yield curve for Treasury bonds, except that the curve will be higher to reflect credit risk and less liquidity.

Default Rate The general level of defaults on corporate bonds is dependent on economic conditions. When the economy is strong, firms generate higher revenue and are better able to cover their debt payments. When the economy is weak, some firms may not generate sufficient revenue to cover their operating and debt expenses and therefore default on their bonds. Exhibit 7.4 shows the default rate on corporate bonds over time. Notice that the default rate was less than 1 percent in the late 1990s when U.S. economic conditions were strong, but it exceeded 3 percent in 2002 when economic conditions were weak.

EXHIBIT 7.4   Default Rate on Corporate Bonds over Time

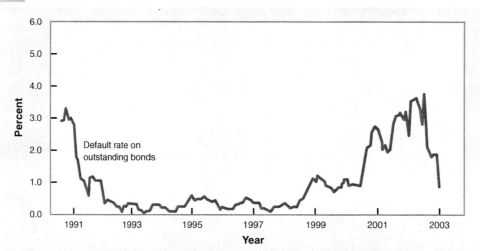

Source: Federal Reserve

Investor Assessment of Risk Since credit risk is associated with corporate bonds, investors may consider purchasing corporate bonds only after assessing the issuing firm's financial condition and ability to cover its debt payments. Thus, investors may rely heavily on financial statements created by the issuing firm. This presents an asymmetric information problem in that the firm knows its true condition, but investors do not. Thus, it can be a challenge for investors to properly assess a firm's ability to cover its debt payments.

ILLUSTRATION Last year, Spectral Insurance Company considered purchasing bonds that were recently issued by Ladron Company. Spectral assessed Ladron's financial statements to determine whether it would have sufficient cash flows in the future to cover its debt payments. In reviewing the revenue and expenses that Ladron reported for the last year, Spectral noticed that Ladron had a large expense categorized as "nonrecurring," which indicates a one-time expense that should not occur again. Spectral ignored those expenses because it wanted to focus only on the typical operating expenses that will occur every year. After estimating Ladron's future cash flows in this manner, Spectral decided that Ladron would be capable of covering its debt payments and purchased bonds issued by Ladron for $20 million.

Last week, Ladron announced that it must file for bankruptcy because it incurred another huge nonrecurring expense this year. Spectral's mistake was that it fully trusted the financial statements reported by Ladron. Like many companies, Ladron classified some operating expenses as "nonrecurring expenses" so that it could reduce its reported operating expenses and increase its reported operating earnings. This is misleading, but may be within accounting guidelines. Nevertheless, Spectral incurred major losses on its investments because of the asymmetric information problem.

Bond Ratings Corporate bonds are rated by rating agencies. Corporate bonds that receive higher ratings can be placed at higher prices (lower yields). Therefore, corporations can achieve a lower cost of financing when their bonds are rated highly. Corporations are especially interested in achieving an investment-grade status on their bonds (medium quality or above) because commercial banks will only invest in bonds that have investment-grade status. A corporate bond's rating may change over time if the issuer's ability to repay the debt changes.

Although bond rating agencies are skilled at assessing ability to repay debt, they are also subject to the asymmetric information problem. They commonly consider the financial statements provided by the issuer of bonds when making their assessment and will not necessarily detect any misleading information contained in the financial statements.

Private Placements of Corporate Bonds

Some corporate bonds are privately placed rather than sold in a public offering. A private placement does not have to be registered with the SEC. Small firms that borrow relatively small amounts of funds (such as $30 million) may consider private placements rather than public offerings, since they may be able to find an institutional investor that will purchase the entire offering. Although the issuer does not need to register with the SEC, it still needs to disclose financial data to convince any prospective purchasers that the bonds will be repaid in a timely manner. The issuer may hire a securities firm to place the bonds because such firms are normally better able to identify institutional investors that may be interested in purchasing privately placed debt.

The institutional investors that commonly purchase a private placement are insurance companies and pension funds. Since privately placed bonds do not have an active secondary market, they are more desirable to institutional investors that are willing to invest for long periods of time.

Characteristics of Corporate Bonds

Corporate bonds can be described according to a variety of characteristics. The bond **indenture** is a legal document specifying the rights and obligations of both the issuing firm and the bondholders. It is very comprehensive (normally several hundred pages) and is designed to address all matters related to the bond issue (collateral, payment dates, default provisions, call provisions, etc.).

Federal law requires that for each bond issue of significant size a **trustee** be appointed to represent the bondholders in all matters concerning the bond issue. The trustee's duties include monitoring the issuing firm's activities to ensure compliance with the terms of the indenture. If the terms are violated, the trustee initiates legal action against the issuing firm and represents the bondholders in that action. Bank trust departments are frequently hired to perform the duties of trustee.

Sinking-Fund Provision Bond indentures frequently include a **sinking-fund provision,** or a requirement that the firm retire a certain amount of the bond issue each year. This provision is considered to be an advantage to the remaining bondholders because it reduces the payments necessary at maturity.

Specific sinking-fund provisions can vary significantly among bond issues. For example, a bond with 20 years until maturity could have a provision to retire 5 percent of the bond issue each year. Or it could have a requirement to retire 5 percent each year beginning in the fifth year, with the remaining amount to be retired at maturity. The actual mechanics of bond retirement are carried out by the trustee.

Protective Covenants Bond indentures normally place restrictions on the issuing firm that are designed to protect the bondholders from being exposed to increasing risk during the investment period. These so-called protective covenants frequently limit the amount of dividends and corporate officers' salaries the firm can pay and also restrict the amount of additional debt the firm can issue. Other financial policies may be restricted as well.

Protective covenants are needed because shareholders and bondholders have different expectations of a firm's management. Shareholders may prefer that managers use a relatively large amount of debt because they can benefit directly from risky managerial decisions that will generate higher returns on investment. In contrast, bondholders simply hope to receive their principal back, with interest. Since they do not share in the excess returns generated by a firm, they would prefer that managerial decisions be conservative. Protective covenants can prevent managers from taking excessive risk and therefore satisfy the preferences of bondholders. If managers are unwilling to accept some protective covenants, they may not be able to obtain debt financing.

Call Provisions Most bonds include a provision allowing the firm to call the bonds. A **call provision** normally requires the firm to pay a price above par value when it calls its bonds. The difference between the bond's call price and par value is the **call premium.** Call provisions have two principal uses. First, if market interest rates decline after a bond issue has been sold, the firm might end up paying a higher rate of interest than the prevailing rate for a long period of time. Under these circumstances, the firm may consider selling a new issue of bonds with a lower interest rate and using the proceeds to retire the previous issue by calling the old bonds.

Second, a call provision may be used to retire bonds as required by a sinking-fund provision. Many bonds have two different call prices: a lower price for calling the bonds to meet sinking-fund requirements and a higher price if the bonds are called for any other reason.

Bondholders normally view a call provision as a disadvantage because it can disrupt their investment plans and reduce their investment returns. As a result, firms must pay slightly higher rates of interest on bonds that are callable, other things being equal.

Bond Collateral Bonds can be classified according to whether they are secured by collateral and by the nature of that collateral. Usually, the collateral is a mortgage on real property (land and buildings). A **first mortgage bond** has first claim on the specified assets. A **chattel mortgage bond** is secured by personal property.

Bonds unsecured by specific property are called **debentures** (backed only by the general credit of the issuing firm). These bonds are normally issued by large, financially sound firms whose ability to service the debt is not in question. **Subordinated debentures** have claims against the firm's assets that are junior to the claims of both mortgage bonds and regular debentures. Owners of subordinated debentures receive nothing until the claims of mortgage bondholders, regular debenture owners, and secured short-term creditors have been satisfied. The main purchasers of subordinated debt are pension funds and insurance companies.

Low- and Zero-Coupon Bonds In the early 1980s, firms began issuing bonds with coupons roughly half the size of the prevailing rate and later issued bonds with zero coupons. These **low-coupon** or **zero-coupon bonds** are therefore issued at a deep discount from par value. Investors are taxed annually on the amount of interest earned, even though much or all of the interest will not be received until maturity. The amount of interest taxed is the amortized discount. (The gain at maturity is prorated over the life of the bond.) Low- and zero-coupon corporate bonds are purchased mainly for tax-exempt investment accounts (pension funds, individual retirement accounts, etc.).

To the issuing firm, these bonds have the advantage of requiring low or no cash outflow during their life. Additionally, the firm is permitted to deduct the amortized discount as interest expense for federal income tax purposes, even though it does not pay interest. This adds to the firm's cash flow. Finally, the demand for low- and zero-coupon bonds has been great enough that firms can, in most cases, issue them at a lower cost than regular bonds.

Variable-Rate Bonds The highly volatile interest rates experienced during the 1970s inspired the development of **variable-rate bonds** (also called floating-rate bonds), which affect the investor and borrower as follows: (1) they allow investors to benefit from rising market interest rates over time, and (2) they allow issuers of bonds to benefit from declining rates over time.

Most issues tie their coupon rate to the London Interbank Offer Rate (LIBOR), the rate at which banks lend funds to each other on an international basis. The rate is typically adjusted every three months.

Variable-rate bonds became very popular in 2004, when interest rates were at low levels. Since most investors presumed that interest rates were likely to rise, they were more willing to purchase variable-rate than fixed-rate bonds. In fact, the volume of variable-rate bonds exceeded that of fixed-rate bonds during this time.

Convertibility Another type of bond, known as a **convertible bond,** allows investors to exchange the bond for a stated number of shares of the firm's common stock. This conversion feature offers investors the potential for high returns if the price of the firm's common stock rises. Investors are therefore willing to accept a lower rate of interest on these bonds, which allows the firm to obtain financing at a lower cost.

Trading Corporate Bonds

Corporate bonds can be traded on an exchange or in the over-the-counter market. More than 2,000 corporate bonds with a market value of more than $2 trillion are traded on the New York Stock Exchange (NYSE). Firms that have their stock listed on the NYSE can list their bonds for free. The bonds listed on the NYSE are traded through its Automated Bond System (ABS), which is an electronic system used by investment firms that are members of the NYSE. The ABS displays prices and matches buy and sell orders.

The number of bonds traded on the NYSE has declined substantially in recent years, as many bonds are now traded in an over-the-counter bond market. Information about the trades in the over-the-counter market is provided by the National Association of Securities Dealers' Trade Reporting and Compliance Engine, which is referred to as "Trace." Some bonds also trade on the American Stock Exchange.

Types of Orders Various bond dealers take positions in corporate bonds and accommodate orders. Individual investors buy or sell corporate bonds through brokers, who communicate the orders to bond dealers. Investors who wish to buy or sell bonds can normally place a **market order;** in this case, the desired transaction will occur at the prevailing market price. Alternatively, they can place a **limit order;** in this case, the transaction will occur only if the price reaches the specified limit. When purchasing bonds, investors use a limit order to specify the maximum limit price they are willing to pay for a bond. When selling bonds, investors use a limit order to specify a minimum limit price at which they are willing to sell their bonds.

Trading Online Corporate bonds are increasingly being traded online. One of the most popular online bond brokerage websites is http://www.Tradebonds.com, which provides bond prices for a large sample of brokers. This site is targeted toward investors who buy in large quantities, but other popular online bond brokerage websites, such as http://www.schwab.com and http://www.etrade.com/global.html, are aimed toward small investors. The pricing of bonds is more transparent online because investors can easily compare the bid and ask spreads among brokers. This transparency has encouraged some brokers to narrow their spreads so that they do not lose business to competitors.

Corporate Bond Quotations

The financial press publishes quotations for corporate bonds, just as it does for Treasury bonds, although in a slightly different format (look back at Exhibit 7.1 to review the format for Treasury bonds). In particular, corporate bond prices are reported in eighths, rather than the thirty-seconds used for Treasury bonds. Thus, a quotation of 101 5/8 for a Disney bond means $101.62 per $100 par value. Corporate bond quotations also typically include the volume of trading, which is normally measured as the number of bonds traded for that day. As in Treasury bond quotations, the yield to maturity is included. A review of bond quotations on any given day will reveal significant differences among the yields of some bonds. These differences may be due to different risk levels, different provisions (such as call features), or different maturities. Bond quotations are typically listed according to the exchange where the bonds trade. Thus, *The Wall Street*

Corporate bond price quotations are provided in *The Wall Street Journal* as shown here. The bonds are listed alphabetically by the name of the issuing corporation. The coupon rate of the bond is shown in the second column and reflects the annual coupon payment as a percentage of the par value. The latest price of each bond is shown in the third column, and

the yield to maturity based on the latest price is shown in the fourth column. The spread is shown in the fifth column, based on the difference between ask and bid prices (measured in basis points, or hundredths of a percent). The trading volume of each bond is provided in the last column.

Corporate Bonds

Monday, August 9, 2004

Forty most active fixed-coupon corporate bonds

COMPANY (TICKER)	COUPON	MATURITY	LAST PRICE	LAST YIELD	*EST SPREAD	UST†	EST $ VOL (000's)
Ford Motor Credit (F)	7.000	Oct 01, 2013	102.880	6.574	232	10	209,079
Ford Motor Credit (F)	7.375	Oct 28, 2009	108.243	5.530	210	5	114,335
Ford Motor Credit (F)	5.625	Oct 01, 2008	102.303	5.000	157	5	97,014
Verizon Wireless Capital LLC (VZW)	5.375	Dec 15, 2006	105.020	3.133	70	2	94,445
Liberty Media (L)	5.700	May 15, 2013	97.767	6.030	177	10	93,005
General Motors (GM)	8.375	Jul 15, 2033	104.250	7.995	294	30	82,367
Comcast Cable Communications Holdings (CMCSA)	8.375	Mar 15, 2013	118.756	5.594	133	10	80,076
DaimlerChrysler North America Holding (DCX)	8.500	Jan 18, 2031	119.753	6.869	182	30	77,200
DaimlerChrysler North America Holding (DCX)	6.500	Nov 15, 2013	106.186	5.632	137	10	76,224
Ford Motor Credit (F)	5.800	Jan 12, 2009	102.439	5.174	175	5	68,607
Wal-Mart Stores (WMT)	6.875	Aug 10, 2009	113.099	3.959	55	5	65,600
Morgan Stanley (MWD)	6.600	Apr 01, 2012	110.506	4.931	68	10	63,297
Ford Motor Credit (F)	7.375	Feb 01, 2011	106.944	6.061	182	10	56,380
Safeway (SWY)	6.500	Mar 01, 2011	108.517	4.961	72	10	54,000
Ford Motor Credit (F)	7.875	Jun 15, 2010	110.167	5.796	238	5	50,613
Walt Disney (DIS)	6.375	Mar 01, 2012	108.756	4.970	72	10	50,366
Associates of North America (C)	6.250	Nov 01, 2008	109.343	3.829	42	5	50,019
Ford Motor (F)	7.450	Jul 16, 2031	96.087	7.799	275	30	49,634
Citigroup (C)	4.250	Jul 29, 2009	101.190	3.983	56	5	48,725
Citigroup (C)	5.125	May 05, 2014	101.023	4.990	74	10	48,470
DaimlerChrysler North America Holding (DCX)	7.750	Jan 18, 2011	114.456	5.086	83	10	42,970
General Electric Capital (GE)	5.450	Jan 15, 2013	104.703	4.765	51	10	42,775
Goldman Sachs Group (GS)	6.875	Jan 15, 2011	112.150	4.664	41	10	42,610
General Motors Acceptance (GM)	6.125	Sep 15, 2006	104.891	3.672	125	2	39,263
General Motors Acceptance (GM)	7.250	Mar 02, 2011	106.171	6.093	186	10	38,713
Merrill Lynch (MER)	4.500	Nov 04, 2010	100.118	4.477	105	5	37,393
Lehman Brothers Holdings (LEH)	7.000	Feb 01, 2008	110.764	3.667	24	5	34,445
J.P. Morgan Chase (JPM)	6.500	Feb 01, 2006	105.647	2.559	13	2	32,742
RBS Capital Trust II (RBS)	6.425	Feb 16, 2034	99.703	6.447	139	30	32,600
Ford Motor Credit (F)	7.600	Aug 01, 2005	104.702	2.654	24	2	32,273
AT&T Wireless Services (AWE)	7.875	Mar 01, 2011	116.260	4.939	70	10	31,510
Target (TGT)	7.000	Jul 15, 2031	116.321	5.795	75	30	31,422
Telus (TCN)	8.000	Jun 01, 2011	115.445	5.267	103	10	30,600
Safeway (SWY)	7.250	Feb 01, 2031	108.810	6.545	150	30	29,800
Goldman Sachs Group (GS)	6.600	Jan 15, 2012	110.437	4.905	66	10	29,797
General Motors (GM)	8.250	Jul 15, 2023	103.758	7.864	281	30	29,713
Halliburton (HAL)-c	3.125	Jul 15, 2023	107.940	1.108	n.a.	n.a.	29,674
Lehman Brothers Holdings (LEH)	6.625	Jan 18, 2012	110.698	4.890	65	10	29,090
Sprint Capital (FON)	8.375	Mar 15, 2012	118.102	5.432	117	10	28,600
Ford Motor (F)	6.625	Oct 01, 2028	88.441	7.684	264	30	28,353
Goldman Sachs Group (GS)	3.875	Jan 15, 2009	99.383	4.028	60	5	28,209

Volume represents total volume for each issue; price/yield data are for trades of $1 million and greater. * Estimated spreads, in basis points (100 basis points is one percentage point), over the 2, 3, 5, 10 or 30-year hot run Treasury note/bond. 2-year: 2.750 07/06; 3-year: 3.125 05/07; 5-year: 3.625 07/09; 10-year: 4.750 05/14; 30-year: 5.375 02/31. †Comparable U.S. Treasury issue. c-Convertible bond.

Source: MarketAxess Corporate BondTicker

Journal lists bonds traded on the NYSE in one section and those traded on the American Stock Exchange in another (although typically on the same page).

Corporate bond price quotations are accessible online at http://www.investinginbonds .com. The quotations can be sorted by maturity, credit rating, coupon rate, or other characteristics.

Junk Bonds

Credit rating agencies assign quality ratings to corporate bonds based on their perceived degree of credit risk. Those bonds that are perceived to have high risk are referred to as **junk bonds.** Junk bonds became popular during the 1980s when firms desired debt financing to finance acquisitions. These firms were attempting to expand without issuing new stock so that profits could ultimately be distributed to existing shareholders. Some of the firms planning to use debt financing were perceived to have high risk, especially given the high proportion of debt in their capital structure. About two-thirds of all junk bond issues are used to finance takeovers (including leveraged buyouts, or LBOs). Some junk bond issues are used by firms to revise their capital structure. The proceeds from issuing bonds are used to repurchase stock, thereby increasing the proportion of debt in the capital structure. Although the newly issued bonds are assigned a low-grade ("junk") quality rating, numerous financial institutions are willing to purchase them because of the relatively high yield offered.

Size of the Junk Bond Market There are currently about 3,700 junk bond offerings in the United States, with a total market value of about $80 billion. This amount represents about 25 percent of the value of all corporate bonds and about 5 percent of the value of all bonds (including Treasury and municipal bonds). About one-third of all junk bonds were once rated higher but have been downgraded to below investment grade. The remaining two-thirds were considered to be below investment-grade quality when they were initially issued.

Participation in the Junk Bond Market There are about 70 large issuers of junk bonds, each with more than $1 billion in debt outstanding. Nextel is the largest issuer, with about $8 billion in debt. The primary investors in junk bonds are mutual funds, life insurance companies, and pension funds. In addition, more than 100 so-called high-yield mutual funds commonly invest in junk bonds. Individuals account for about one-tenth of all investors in the junk bond market. Recently, some issuers of junk bonds have attempted to attract more individual investors by lowering the minimum denomination to $1,000. High-yield mutual funds allow individual investors to invest in a diversified portfolio of junk bonds with a small investment.

The secondary market for junk bonds in the United States is facilitated by about 20 bond traders (or market makers) that make a market for junk bonds. That is, they execute secondary market transactions for customers and also invest in junk bonds for their own account.

Risk Premium of Junk Bonds Junk bonds offer high yields that contain a risk premium to compensate investors for the high risk. Typically, the premium is between 3 percent and 7 percent above Treasury bonds with the same maturity. Exhibit 7.5 compares the yields offered by junk (high-yield) bonds versus BBB- and AA-rated bonds. The difference in yields for the various types of bond is primarily attributed to a difference in risk. First, notice that at any point in time the difference between the yields offered by junk bonds versus BBB-rated bonds is larger than the difference in yields between the BBB- and

EXHIBIT 7.5 Comparison of Yields of Junk Bonds versus other Bonds

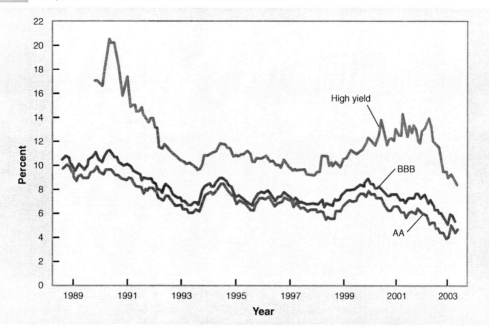

Note. The data are monthly averages through October 2003 provided by the Federal Reserve. The AA and BBB rates are calculated from bonds in the Merrill Lynch AA index and BBB index, respectively, with seven to ten years of maturity remaining. The high-yield rate is the yield on the Merrill Lynch 175 high-yield index.

AA-rated bonds. Second, notice that the difference between the yields of junk bonds versus BBB-rated bonds changes over time. During periods of weak economies, such as 1990–1991 and 2001–2002, the difference is larger. Although investors always require a higher yield on junk bonds than bonds rated BBB or above, they require a higher premium during weak economies when there is a greater likelihood that the issuer will not generate sufficient cash flows to cover the debt payments.

Performance of Junk Bonds Junk bonds are generally perceived to offer high returns with high risk. During the mid-1980s, junk bond defaults were relatively infrequent, which may have renewed public interest in them and encouraged corporations to issue more.

After the stock market crash of October 1987, the market became more concerned about the risk of junk bonds. Issuers had to lower the price to compensate for the higher perceived risk. The junk bond market received another blow in the late 1980s, when insider trading charges were filed against Drexel Burnham Lambert, Inc., the main dealer in the market, for violating various regulations.

In the early 1990s, the popularity of junk bonds declined as a result of three key factors. First, there were allegations of insider trading against some participants in the junk bond market. Second, the financial problems of a few major issuers of junk bonds scared some investors away. Third, the financial problems in the thrift industry caused regulators to regulate investments by thrifts more closely. The Financial Institutions Reform, Recovery, and Enforcement Act (FIRREA) mandated that savings institutions liquidate their investments in junk bonds. Because savings institutions controlled about 7 percent of the junk bond market, there was additional downward pressure on prices. Although these institutions were given five years to liquidate their junk bonds to alleviate this pressure on prices, many thrifts liquidated their bonds within a few months after the FIRREA was enacted.

During the late-1990s, junk bonds performed very well, and there were few defaults. Consequently, junk bonds became popular once again. However, the defaults increased during the 2001–2002 period when economic conditions were weak.

Contagion Effects in the Junk Bond Market Investors may be systematically discouraged from investment in junk bonds by specific adverse information, which means that the junk bond market is susceptible to **contagion effects.** Many firms that issue junk bonds have excessive debt service payments and may possibly experience cash flow deficiencies if sales are less than anticipated. Thus, they are all susceptible to a single underlying event, such as an economic downturn. Furthermore, media reports about a single well-known firm that may be unable to service its junk bond payments can cause increased concern (whether justified or not) about other highly leveraged firms. Such concern can encourage investors to sell holdings of junk bonds or discourage other investors from purchasing junk bonds.

How Corporate Bonds Facilitate Restructuring

http://bonds.yahoo.com/glossary1.html Provides a glossary of common terms used in the bond market.

Firms can issue corporate bonds to finance the restructuring of their assets and to restructure their capital structure. Such restructuring can have a major impact on the firm's degree of financial leverage, the potential return to shareholders, the risk to shareholders, and the risk to bondholders.

Using Bonds to Finance a Leveraged Buyout A leveraged buyout (LBO) is typically financed with senior debt (such as debentures and collateralized loans) and subordinated debt. The senior debt accounts for 50 to 60 percent of LBO financing on average.

LBO activity increased dramatically in the late 1980s, when it was more than double the level in the early 1960s. In 1988, there were more than 100 LBOs in which a publicly held firm was taken private. The premium paid when repurchasing shares to execute an LBO typically ranged between 30 percent and 40 percent above the prevailing market price. This suggests that the investors conducting the LBO believed that the firm was substantially undervalued when it was publicly held. Their expectation was that by reducing the equity interest of the firm down to a small group of people (possibly management and other employees), managerial efficiency of the firm would increase. The costs of monitoring to ensure that management's decisions are in the best interests of the shareholders are negligible when management owns all of the stock.

Although LBOs may possibly enhance managerial efficiency, they raised concerns about corporate debt levels. During the 1980s, corporate debt of U.S. firms increased substantially. The impact of the recession in the early 1990s on corporate performance may have been more pronounced because of the high degree of financial leverage.

The best-known LBO was the $24.7 billion buyout of RJRNabisco, Inc. by Kohlberg Kravis Roberts, Inc. (KKR) in 1988. KKR's equity investment was only about $1.4 billion, less than 6 percent of the purchase price. The debt financing was primarily composed of long-term bonds and bank loans. Before the acquisition, RJR's long-term debt was less than its shareholders' equity. After the acquisition, RJR's long-term debt was more than 12 times its shareholders' equity. Annual interest expenses were expected to be more than five times what they were before the acquisition. In 1988, RJR's cash flows totaled $1.8 billion, which was not expected to be sufficient to meet interest payments on the debt. Thus, the company needed additional cash flow to accommodate the substantial

The Wall Street Journal provides the following information related to this chapter on a daily basis:

- Price quotations on corporate bonds traded on the New York Stock Exchange and American Stock Exchange.
- Price quotations on Treasury bonds and notes, and on bonds issued by other government agencies (see "Treas./Gov't. Issues").
- Recent price trends in debt markets (see "Credit Markets"). This section explains major changes in the prices and also provides a yield curve based on Treasury securities with different maturities.
- Firms that have issued new debt securities (see "New Securities Issues").
- Price information on bonds of various types of issuers. An example is shown here. Percentage changes in the bond prices are shown since the previous day, since the beginning of the year, and over a 12-month period. This table can be used to compare price changes across different types of bonds.

Major Bond Indexes

	CLOSE	NET CHG	% CHG	52-WEEK HIGH	52-WEEK LOW	52-WEEK % CHG	YTD % CHG
U.S. Treasury Securities Lehman Brothers							
Intermediate	7645.15	+0.08	+0.00	7734.54	7323.99	+4.06	+2.01
Long-term	12353.14	+5.24	+0.04	12758.67	11198.53	+9.11	+3.81
Composite	8696.14	+1.08	+0.01	8852.48	8201.40	+5.58	+2.55
Broad Market Lehman Brothers (preliminary)							
U.S. Aggregate	1082.79	+0.88	+0.07	1094.87	1016.47	+4.76	+2.10
U.S. Gov't/Credit	1252.43	+0.84	+0.06	1275.99	1175.53	+4.77	+1.93
U.S. Corporate Debt Issues Merrill Lynch							
Corporate Master	1469.23	+1.05	+0.07	1494.43	1363.44	+7.63	+2.12
High Yield	673.24	-0.02	-0.00	673.91	583.00	+14.98	+3.10
Yankee Bonds	1071.63	+0.73	+0.07	1088.87	1007.29	+6.29	+2.10
Mortgage-Backed Securities current coupon; Merrill Lynch; Dec. 31, 1986=100							
Ginnie Mae	435.11	+0.53	+0.12	436.04	403.10	+7.91	+3.29
Fannie Mae	434.85	+0.53	+0.12	439.19	406.04	+7.08	+2.35
Freddie Mac	266.16	+0.16	+0.06	268.83	247.66	+7.45	+2.59
Tax-Exempt Securities Merrill Lynch; Dec. 22, 1999							
6% Bond Buyer Muni	110.50	-0.09	-0.08	133.88	104.94	+4.37	-1.56
7-12 Yr G.O.	199.46	-0.12	-0.06	202.96	184.05	+8.03	+1.96
12-22 Yr G.O.	211.02	-0.06	-0.03	216.41	192.36	+9.28	+1.88
22+ Yr Revenue	197.32	-0.11	-0.06	203.97	181.96	+8.33	+0.57

increase in financial leverage. As a result of the increase in financial leverage, prices of RJR bonds declined by 20 percent when the LBO was announced. After the LBO, RJR attempted to sell various businesses to improve its cash position.

It is of interest to note that RJR issued stock to reduce its degree of financial leverage in 1990 and again in 1991. Nabisco has since been sold by RJR. Many other firms with excessive financial leverage resulting from a previous LBO also reissued stock in the 1990s. They typically used some of the proceeds from the stock issuance to retire some outstanding debt, thereby reducing their periodic interest payments on debt. This process was more feasible for firms that could issue shares of stock for high prices because the proceeds would retire a larger amount of outstanding debt.

Using Bonds to Revise the Capital Structure Corporations commonly issue bonds in order to revise their capital structure. If they believe that they will have sufficient cash flows to cover their debt payments, they may consider using more debt and less equity, which implies a higher degree of financial leverage. Debt is normally perceived to be a cheaper source of capital than equity, as long as the corporation has the ability to meet its debt payments. Furthermore, a high degree of financial leverage allows the earnings of the firm to be distributed to a smaller group of shareholders. In some cases, corporations

EXHIBIT 7.6   Participation of Financial Institutions in Bond Markets

Financial Institution	Participation in Bond Markets
Commercial banks and savings and loan associations (S&Ls)	• Purchase bonds for their asset portfolio. • Sometimes place municipal bonds for municipalities. • Sometimes issue bonds as a source of secondary capital.
Finance companies	• Commonly issue bonds as a source of long-term funds.
Mutual funds	• Use funds received from the sale of shares to purchase bonds. Some bond mutual funds specialize in particular types of bonds, while others invest in all types.
Brokerage firms	• Facilitate bond trading by matching up buyers and sellers of bonds in the secondary market.
Investment banking firms	• Place newly issued bonds for governments and corporations. They may place the bonds and assume the risk of market price uncertainty or place the bonds on a best-efforts basis in which they do not guarantee a price for the issuer.
Insurance companies	• Purchase bonds for their asset portfolio.
Pension funds	• Purchase bonds for their asset portfolio.

issue bonds and use the proceeds to repurchase some of their existing stock. This strategy is referred to as a debt-for-equity swap.

When corporations use an excessive amount of debt, they may be unable to make their debt payments. Consequently, they may revise their capital structure by reducing their level of debt. In an equity-for-debt swap, corporations issue stock and use the proceeds to retire existing debt.

Institutional Use of Bond Markets

http://www.bloomberg.com
Yield curves of major countries' government securities.

All financial institutions participate in the bond markets, as summarized in Exhibit 7.6. Commercial banks, bond mutual funds, insurance companies, and pension funds are dominant participants in the bond market activity on any given day. A financial institution's investment decisions will often simultaneously affect bond market and other financial market activity. For example, an institution that anticipates higher interest rates may sell its bond holdings and purchase either money market securities or stocks. Conversely, financial institutions that expect lower interest rates may shift investments from their money market securities and/or stock portfolios to their bond portfolio.

Globalization of Bond Markets

GL🌐BALASPECTS   In recent years, financial institutions such as pension funds, insurance companies, and commercial banks have commonly purchased foreign bonds. For example, pension funds of General Electric, United Technologies Corporation, and IBM frequently invest in foreign bonds with the intention of achieving higher returns for their employees. Many public pension funds also invest in foreign bonds for the same reason. Because of the frequent cross-border investments in bonds, the bond markets have become increasingly integrated among countries. In addition, mutual funds containing U.S. securities are accessible to foreign investors.

Primary dealers of U.S. Treasury notes and bonds have opened offices in London, Tokyo, and other foreign cities to accommodate the foreign demand for these securities.

http://bonds.yahoo.com
Summary of bond market
activity and analysis of
bond market conditions.

When the U.S. markets close, markets in Hong Kong and Tokyo are opening. As these markets close, European markets are opening. The U.S. market opens as markets in London and other European cities are closing. Thus, the prices of U.S. Treasury bonds at the time the U.S. market opens may differ substantially from the previous day's closing price.

In recent years, low-quality bonds have been issued globally by governments and large corporations. These bonds are referred to as **global junk bonds.** The demand for these bonds has been high as some institutional investors are attracted to their high yields. For example, corporate bonds have been issued by Klabin (Brazil) and Cementos Mexicanos (Mexico), while government bonds have been issued by Brazil, Mexico, Venezuela, the Czech Republic, and Spain.

The global development of the bond market is primarily attributed to the bond offerings by country governments. In general, bonds issued by foreign governments (referred to as sovereign bonds) are attractive to investors because of the government's ability to meet debt obligations. Nevertheless, some country governments have defaulted on their bonds, including Argentina (1982, 1989, 1990, 2001), Brazil (1986, 1989, 1991), Costa Rica (1989), Russia and other former Soviet republics (1993, 1998), and the former Yugoslavia (1992). Given that sovereign bonds are exposed to credit risk, credit ratings are assigned to them by Moody's and Standard & Poor's. Rating agencies tend to disagree more about the credit risk of sovereign bonds than about bonds issued by U.S. corporations. Perhaps this is due to a lack of consistent information available for country governments, which results in more arbitrary ratings. Also, the process of rating specific countries is still relatively new.

Eurobond Market

In 1963, U.S.-based corporations were limited to the amount of funds they could borrow in the United States for overseas operations. Consequently, these corporations began to issue bonds in the so-called Eurobond market, where bonds denominated in various currencies were placed. The U.S. dollar is used the most, denominating 70 to 75 percent of the Eurobonds.

Non-U.S. investors who desire dollar-denominated bonds may use the Eurobond market if they prefer bearer bonds to the registered corporate bonds issued in the United States. Alternatively, they may use the Eurobond market because they are more familiar with bond placements within their own country.

An underwriting syndicate of investment banks participates in the Eurobond market by placing the bonds issued. It normally underwrites the bonds, guaranteeing a particular value to be received by the issuer. Thus, the syndicate is exposed to underwriting risk, or the risk that it will be unable to sell the bonds above the price that it guaranteed the issuer.

The issuer of Eurobonds can choose the currency in which the bonds are denominated. The issuer's periodic coupon payments and repayment of principal will normally be in this currency. Moreover, the financing cost from issuing bonds depends on the currency chosen. In some cases, a firm may denominate the bonds in a currency with a low interest rate and use earnings generated by one of its subsidiaries to cover the payments. For example, the coupon rate on a Eurobond denominated in Swiss francs may be 5 percentage points lower than a dollar-denominated bond. A U.S. firm may consider issuing Swiss franc–denominated bonds and converting the francs to dollars for use in the United States. Then it could instruct a subsidiary in Switzerland to cover the periodic coupon payments with earnings that the subsidiary generates. In this way, a lower financing rate would be achieved without exposure to exchange rate risk.

SUMMARY

- Bonds can be classified in four categories according to the type of issuer: Treasury bonds, federal agency bonds, municipal bonds, and corporate bonds. The issuers are perceived to have different levels of credit risk. In addition, the bonds have different degrees of liquidity and different provisions. Thus, quoted yields at a given point in time vary across bonds.

- Many institutional investors, such as commercial banks, insurance companies, pension funds, and

bond mutual funds, are major investors in bonds. These institutional investors adjust their holdings of bonds in response to expectations of future interest rates.

- Bond yields vary among countries. Investors are attracted to high bond yields in foreign countries, causing funds to flow to those countries. Consequently, bond markets have become globally integrated.

POINT COUNTER-POINT

Should Financial Institutions Invest in Junk Bonds?

Point Yes. Financial institutions have managers who are capable of weighing the risk against the potential return. They can earn a significantly higher return when investing in junk bonds than the return on Treasury bonds. Their shareholders benefit when they increase the return on the portfolio.

Counter-Point No. The financial system is based on trust in financial institutions and confidence that the finan-

cial institutions will survive. If financial institutions take excessive risk, the entire financial system is at risk.

Who Is Correct? Use InfoTrac or some other source search engine to learn more about this issue. Offer your own opinion on this issue.

QUESTIONS AND APPLICATIONS

1. **Bond Indenture** What is a bond indenture? What is the function of a trustee, as related to the bond indenture?

2. **Sinking-Fund Provision** Explain the use of a sinking-fund provision. How can it reduce the investor's risk?

3. **Protective Covenants** What are protective covenants? Why are they needed?

4. **Call Provisions** Explain the call provision of bonds. How can it affect the price of a bond?

5. **Bond Collateral** Explain the use of bond collateral, and identify the common types of collateral for bonds.

6. **Debentures** What are debentures? How do they differ from subordinated debentures?

7. **Zero-Coupon Bonds** What are the advantages and disadvantages to a firm that issues low- or zero-coupon bonds?

8. **Variable-Rate Bonds** Are variable-rate bonds attractive to investors who expect interest rates to decrease? Explain. Would a firm consider variable-rate bonds if it expected that interest rates will decrease? Explain.

9. **Convertible Bonds** Why can convertible bonds be issued by firms at a higher price than other bonds?

10. **Global Interaction of Bond Yields** Assume that bond yields in Japan rise. How might U.S. bond yields be affected? Why?

11. **Impact of FIRREA on the Junk Bond Market** Explain how the Financial Institutions Reform, Recovery

and Enforcement Act (FIRREA) could have affected the market value of junk bonds.

12. **Calling Bonds** As a result of September 11, 2001, economic conditions were expected to decline. How do you think this would have affected the tendency of firms to call bonds?

13. **Yield Curve for Municipal Securities** Explain how the shape of the yield curve for municipal securities compares to the Treasury yield curve. Under what conditions do you think the two yield curves could be different?

14. **Bond Downgrade** Explain how the downgrading of bonds for a particular corporation affects the corporation, the investors that currently hold these bonds, and other investors who may invest in the bonds in the near future.

15. **Junk Bonds** Merrito Inc. is a large U.S. firm that issued bonds several years ago. Its bond ratings declined over time, and about a year ago, the bonds were rated in the junk bond classification. Nevertheless, investors were buying the bonds in the secondary market because of the attractive yield they offered. Last week, Merrito defaulted on its bonds, and the prices of most other junk bonds declined abruptly on the same day. Explain why news of the financial problems of Merrito Inc. could cause the prices of junk bonds issued by other firms to decrease, even when those firms had no business relationships with Merrito. Explain why the prices of those junk bonds with less liquidity declined more than those with a high degree of liquidity.

16. **Event Risk** An insurance company purchased bonds issued by Hartnett Company two years ago. Today, Hartnett Company has begun to issue junk bonds and is using the funds to repurchase most of its existing stock. Why might the market value of those bonds held by the insurance company be affected by this action?

Interpret the following statements made by Wall Street analysts and portfolio managers:

a. "The values of some stocks are dependent on the bond market. When investors are not interested in junk bonds, the values of stocks ripe for leveraged buyouts decline."

b. "The recent trend in which many firms are using debt to repurchase some of their stock is a good strategy as long as they can withstand the stagnant economy."

c. "Although yields among bonds are related, today's rumors of a tax cut caused an increase in the yield on municipal bonds, while the yield on corporate bonds declined."

Assess today's risk premiums on industrial bonds, using the website http://www.bondsonline.com. Click on "Corporate bond spreads" and then on "Industrials."

What is the risk premium on AA-rated bonds with a 30-year maturity? What is the risk premium on BBB-rated bonds with a 30-year maturity? What is the risk premium on CCC-rated bonds with a 30-year maturity? Given the prevailing economic conditions, which of these three categories of bonds would be the best investment (in your opinion)?

Forecasting Bond Returns As a portfolio manager for an insurance company, you are about to invest funds in one of three possible investments: (1) 10-year coupon bonds issued by the U.S. Treasury, (2) 20-year zero-coupon bonds issued by the Treasury, or (3) one-year Treasury securities. Each possible investment is perceived to have no risk of default. You plan to maintain this investment for a one-year period. The return of each investment over a one-year horizon will be about the same if interest rates do not change over the next year. However, you anticipate that the U.S. inflation rate will decline substantially over the next year, while most of the other portfolio managers in the United States expect inflation to increase slightly.

a. If your expectations are correct, how will the return of each investment be affected over the one-year horizon?

b. If your expectations are correct, which of the three investments should have the highest return over the one-year horizon? Why?

c. Offer one reason why you might not select the investment that would have the highest expected return over the one-year investment horizon.

PROBLEMS

1. **Inflation-Indexed Treasury Bond** An inflation-indexed Treasury bond has a par value of $1,000 and a coupon rate of 6 percent. An investor purchases this bond and holds it for one year. During the year, the consumer price index increases by 1 percent every six months, for a total increase in inflation of 2 percent. What are the total interest payments the investor will receive during the year?

2. **Inflation-Indexed Treasury Bond** Assume that the U.S. economy experienced deflation during the year and that the consumer price index decreased by 1 percent in the first six months of the year and by 2 percent during the second six months of the year. If an investor had purchased inflation-indexed Treasury bonds with a par value of $10,000 and a coupon rate of 5 percent, how much would she have received in interest during the year?

FLOW OF FUNDS EXERCISE

Financing in the Bond Markets

If the economy continues to be strong, Carson may need to increase its production capacity by about 50 percent over the next few years to satisfy demand. It would need financing to expand and accommodate the increase in production. Recall that the yield curve is currently upward sloping. Also recall that Carson is concerned about a possible slowing of the economy because of potential Fed actions to reduce inflation. It needs funding to cover payments for supplies. It is also considering the issuance of stock or bonds to raise funds in the next year.

a. Assume that Carson has two choices to satisfy the increased demand for its products. It could increase production by 10 percent with its existing facilities. In this case, it could obtain short-term financing to cover the extra production expense and then use a portion of the revenue received to finance this level of production in the future. Alternatively, it could issue bonds and use the proceeds to buy a larger facility that would allow for 50 percent more capacity.

b. Carson currently has a large amount of debt, and its assets have already been pledged to back up its existing debt. It does not have additional collateral. At this point in time, the credit risk premium it would pay is similar in the short-term and long-term debt markets. Does this imply that the cost of financing is the same in both markets?

c. Should Carson consider using a call provision if it issues bonds? Why? Why might Carson decide not to include a call provision on the bonds?

d. If Carson issues bonds, it would be a relatively small bond offering. Should Carson consider a private placement of bonds? What type of investor might be interested in participating in a private placement? Do you think Carson could offer the same yield on a private placement as it could on a public placement? Explain.

e. Financial institutions such as insurance companies and pension funds commonly purchase bonds. Explain the flow of funds that runs through these financial institutions and ultimately reaches corporations such as Carson Company that issue bonds.

WSJ EXERCISE

Impact of Treasury Financing on Bond Prices

The Treasury periodically issues new bonds to finance the deficit. Review recent issues of *The Wall Street Journal* or check related online news to find a recent article on such financing. Does the article suggest that financial markets are expecting upward pressure on interest rates as a result of the Treasury financing? What happened to prices of existing bonds when the Treasury announced its intentions to issue new bonds?

index

index

index

index

index